W9-ATE-635

Bureaucracy, Innovation, and Public Policy

Bureaucracy, Innovation, and Public Policy

George W. Downs, Jr.
University of California, Davis

Lexington Books
D.C. Heath and Company
Lexington, Massachusetts
Toronto

Library of Congress Cataloging in Publication Data

Downs, George W.
  Bureaucracy, innovation and public policy.

  Bibliography: p.
  1. Juvenile corrections—United States—States. 2. Community-
based corrections—United States—States. 3. Bureaucracy—
Case studies. 4. Diffusion of innovations—United States—
States—Case studies. I. Title.
HV9104.D7   364.6   76-19148
ISBN 0-669-00872-9

Copyright © 1976 by D.C. Heath and Company

All rights reserved. No part of this publication may be reproduced or
transmitted in any form or by any means, electronic or mechanical, including photocopy, recording, or any information storage or retrieval system,
without permission in writing from the publisher.

Published simultaneously in Canada

Printed in the United States of America

International Standard Book Number: 0-669-00872-9

Library of Congress Catalog Card Number: 76-19148

364.6
D75

78-662

To Bruce and Cari René—
the least I can offer

Contents

List of Figures

List of Tables

Preface

The task of unravelling the determinants of public policy is one that has preoccupied social scientists since the advent of the behavioral revolution of the 1960s. This book attempts to contribute to this effort by systematically exploring the impact of bureaucracies and their environments on the adoption of policy innovations. In the course of this exploration it seeks to explain why comparative policy research has so far been unable to achieve its objective of formulating a satisfactory positive theory of policy formation, as well as why innovation research has been plagued by seemingly contradictory findings. For purposes of illustration, the adoption and implementation of a recent and widely heralded policy innovation in the field of juvenile corrections is studied in considerable detail.

Writing this book has afforded me the opportunity to become indebted to a host of generous individuals. Larry Mohr and Robert Vinter provided a wealth of encouragement and insightful criticism from its inception to its completion. Irwin Epstein, George Greenberg, Jack Walker and numerous individuals connected with Michigan's Institute of Public Policy Studies rendered valuable assistance at a number of crucial junctures.

Rosemary Sarri, Paul Isenstadt, and the staff of the National Assessment of Juvenile Corrections contributed, both by participating in data collection and in helping to familiarize me with the field of juvenile corrections. Two of my colleagues on the project—John Hall and Garry Kemp—logged countless air miles and unremunerated overtime during the six-month period in which we visited every state capital. I thank them for their conscientiousness and unflagging good humor. Vann Jones simultaneously functioned as typist and editor through several manuscript drafts. His knowledge, patience, and meticulousness are awesome.

I would also like to express my appreciation for the cooperation of the directors of the fifty state juvenile corrections agencies, their staffs, and the numerous other public officials who permitted themselves to be interviewed at great length. Despite their overexposure to academics, the vast majority were helpful, frank, and interested in, as well as tolerant of, our efforts.

Data collection and analysis were carried out in conjunction with the National Assessment of Juvenile Corrections project supported by a grant (75NI–99–0010) from the Juvenile Justice and Delinquency Prevention Operations Task Group, Law Enforcement Assistance Administration, U.S. Department of Justice, under authorizing legislation of the Omnibus Crime Control and Safe Streets Act of 1968 and the Juvenile Justice and Delinquency Prevention Act of 1974. Of course, the grantor's financial support does not necessarily indicate concurrence with the statements or conclusions made by the author, who takes full responsibility for the contents.

Introduction

Despite the saliency of both bureaucracy and public policy, there is a conspicuous and unfortunate absence of systematic and quantitative research that attempts to link the two. Investigations into the impact of bureaucracy on policy, whether in the mainstream of academic political science or primarily intended as polemical exposé, have usually taken place within the context of single or multiple case studies. Coming from a different tradition, quantitative research into the determinants of public policy has, for reasons that will be explored subsequently, consistently neglected to include independent variables that represent characteristics of bureaucracies, their environments, or bureaucratic politics (one category of the interaction between the two).

This book reports on one attempt to partially remedy this situation in connection with an extremely important subset of public policies—policy innovations. These consist of policies new to the political units (here states) adopting them no matter how long they may have been around or how many comparable units may have adopted them [Walker, 1969:88]. While no clear, unambiguous criteria exist for distinguishing policy innovations from any minor modification in current practices, the label is normally applied only to policies that represent significant, unprecedented, and qualitative departures from past policies. This emphasis makes it possible to differentiate between policy innovations and policies that incrementally alter some characteristic of an already existing policy (e.g., one that increases the level of state aid to schools) or that restore a previous status quo (e.g., reinstitution of capital punishment). Fairly recent examples of policy innovations at the state level have been program budgeting, affirmative action programs, and the employment of paraprofessionals in welfare agencies.

The major premise of what follows is that the bureaucracies potentially responsible for implementing such innovations, and their immediate task environments, play significant roles in determining states' adoptive behavior and that these roles are not simply reflections of states' socioeconomic environments. This creates the expectation that a knowledge of key bureaucratic and task-environmental characteristics will substantially increase our ability to understand and predict how states will react to policy innovations beyond what would be possible on the basis of a thorough knowledge of their socioeconomic development alone—or on the basis of their political attributes, for that matter. Thus a primary goal will be to investigate, in connection with a specific policy innovation, the extent to which a focus on the bureaucracy and its task environment increases the amount of variance we are capable of explaining.

All this will be handled within a context of trying to assess—logically as well as empirically—the capacity of public policy and innovation theory to identify the principal determinants of the adoption of policy innovations and illuminate the processes involved. This entails extensive and frequent references to the public policy and innovation research literatures: diverse findings must be compared and evaluated; potentially relevant dimensions of the socioeconomic and task environments and the bureaucracy must be sorted out and operationalized; implicit hypotheses and theoretical arguments must be made explicit; and so forth. This sort of analysis is tedious, but it is necessary in order to fully understand the implications of the empirical findings that will be presented. It is also hoped that this exercise will result in a better understanding of the present state of the art and, more importantly, of the direction research might profitably take.

In what follows, the focus will be on a single policy innovation: deinstitutionalization in juvenile corrections. In the simplest terms, deinstitutionalization is a policy by which the treatment of juvenile offenders is shifted from relatively large, isolated, and closed institutions or training schools to smaller, open, community-based settings through which their reintegration into the community can be facilitated.[a] It is among the most significant and controversial policy innovations in the area of juvenile corrections.

The data that will be presented were collected in connection with research by the National Assessment of Juvenile Corrections into the sources of variation in correctional policy outputs among the fifty states. Data collection began with several "sensitizing" field trips to state capitals; these were followed by exploratory case studies (of approximately fifteen man-days each) conducted in sixteen states; and the final stage consisted of structured interviews with correctional executives and the analysis of statistical records in all fifty states. This research strategy permitted the blending of a traditional case study approach with a more systematic, quantitative one. The case study phase provided an invaluable opportunity to become familiar with the actors, processes, and issues central to policy making in the field of juvenile corrections—an area where virtually no previous research had been conducted. From the information and impressions gathered through these studies, a lengthy, structured interview schedule and statistical data instrument were developed to systematically collect data on policy outputs and those characteristics of the bureaucracy, its personnel, and its task environment that were thought to have an impact on them. To this core data set were later

---

[a]Movements toward deinstitutionalization are also taking place in mental health and, to a lesser extent, in adult corrections.

added numerous variables extracted from Census Bureau publications and the comparative state policy analysis literature.

The many attributes of "deinstitutionalization rate" as a dependent variable (both methodological and theoretical) will be enumerated and discussed in Chapter 2, but it is particularly well suited as the object for research into the impact of bureaucracy on public policy. It is comparably perceived across the states in terms of its fundamental characteristics, and its implementation looks the same in Georgia as it does in Oregon. The exploratory case studies in sixteen states revealed that in terms of agenda setting and implementation—the two major mechanisms by which the bureaucracy is usually viewed as molding policy—action on the part of the bureaucracy was the sine qua non of a state's adopting the policy of deinstitutionalization. Of course, this is insufficient evidence upon which to infer bureaucratic hegemony even in this single instance. It could well be that the bureaucracy although playing a pivotal role as the locus of critical policy decisions was only the proximate cause of adoption. Much of the analysis that follows is an attempt to provisionally disentangle the relative proportions in which characteristics of the bureaucracy seem to determine policy independently or merely reflect the network of environmental motivations and constraints in which they exist.

This study is exploratory in both a theoretical and empirical sense. In trying simultaneously to understand what determined the variation in the adoption of a single policy innovation across the fifty states and to offer some tentative observations about public policy and innovation in public organizations, as much emphasis has been placed on logical analysis—attempting to make new connections and further distinctions, employing different perspectives, and so forth—as on data analysis. One cannot help but feel that one of the reasons there have been so many seemingly contradictory empirical findings in these fields is that relatively little effort has been expended in trying to think through *why* we expect a certain variable like centralization or socioeconomic development to be positively related to innovation, whether these terms are, in fact, unidimensional, and under what conditions we expect the relationships to alter. Single-minded concentration on achieving a high percentage of explained variance can be unwise. As Herbert Simon [1968:454] has said:

We should not be unduly impressed by excellent statistical fits of data to theory. More important than whether the data fit is why they fit—i.e., what components in the theory are critical to the goodness of fit. To answer this question, we must analyse the internal structure of the theory.

Although the best work in public policy and innovation has frequently been done in connection with empirical studies, few notable contributions have been realized by anything remotely approaching classical hypothesis testing. Data analysis has been used in order to *generate* or extract hypotheses, not simply to "test" them, and this is how it will be employed here. Actually, there is some question whether a more "formal" approach really exists.

In most formal theories of induction, particularly those that belong to the genus "hypothetico-deductive" or "H-D," hypotheses spring full-blown from the head of Zeus, then are tested with data that exist timelessly and quite independently of the hypotheses . . . . It was one of Norwood Hanson's important contributions to challenge this separation of hypothesis from data, and to demonstrate that in the history of science the retroduction of generalizations and explanations from data has become one of the central and crucial processes [Simon, 1968:455–56].

At any rate, the sorts of questions with which this essay is concerned, and the state of the art, appear to call for a process of quasi-inferential analysis that differs from a more formal deductive or axiomatic approach in the degree of explicit interaction that takes place between theory and data in the process of hypothesis generation, as well as by its movement toward rather than from increased abstraction. It also differs from "grounded theory" [Glaser and Strauss, 1967] in its emphasis on the logical exploration of hypotheses in terms of consistency, generalizability, and so forth. Whether or not this method produces the elusive grail of middle-range theory is a question this author shall leave to those who can define it.

The tentative and exploratory character of what follows is a function of data limitations as well as of the author's perspective. For various reasons a cross-sectional design had to be employed, and the data suffer from the attendant drawbacks. An effort was made to minimize these by probing for sources of disequilibrium. When gathering information about the backgrounds of staff, for instance, we sought to discover how constant the distribution of certain key attributes had remained over the past five years. In addition, the preliminary case studies carried out in sixteen states afforded us the opportunity to conduct extended open-ended interviews with a variety of insiders about the evolution of juvenile corrections policy in their states. Hopefully the knowledge gained from these interviews was able to enlighten interpretation of the empirical findings. All of this did not magically transform the data from cross-sectional to longitudinal, but it helps make the best out of a basically unsatisfactory situation. At the very least, it served to indicate where the deficiencies were likely to lie—that is, to point where inferences were riskiest. Another major limitation of the data involves the measurement of variables. This problem is endemic to all such research, and nothing more will be said at this point other than that an effort will be made to draw attention to variables that are particularly unsatisfying operationalizations, whose measurement at the ordinal or interval level is markedly questionable, or upon which the distributions are severely skewed.

This promise to draw attention to the pockmarks of the research springs from a belief that visibly struggling with caveats, provisional distinctions, and so forth is likely to produce a greater theoretical payoff than the hidden deletions, chopping, and blending that are necessary to create a deceptively clean and parsimonious study. Moreover, it is a matter of personal disposition: This sort of exploration is more enjoyable. Robert Nozick [1974:xii] sums up the entire matter rather nicely, in a quite different context:

The word "exploration" is appropriately chosen. One view about how to write a philosophy book holds that an author should think through all of the details of the view he presents, and its problems, polishing and refining his view to present to the world a finished, complete, and elegant whole. This is not my view. At any rate, I believe that there is also a place and a function in our ongoing intellectual life for a less complete work, containing unfinished presentations, conjectures, open questions and problems, leads, side connections, as well as the main line of argument. There is room for words on subjects other than last words.

A few words should be said about the organization of this volume. Chapters 1 and 2 deal with the intellectual antecedents of the research and the areas of study to which some contribution might hopefully be made. The first chapter is an extended discussion of past research on the determinants of public policy. It investigates why this research has failed to fulfill its objective of formulating a positive theory of policy formation and presents the rationale for studying the role of the bureaucracy and its environment in determining policy outputs. In addition, it summarizes the implications of previous research for data analysis and the type of models that should be constructed.

Chapter 2 focuses on research on the adoption and diffusion of innovations concurrent with a description of the dependent variable. The former is necessary not only because what follows deals with a policy that is also an innovation, but because the policy-determinants literature provides no guidance in selecting those characteristics of the bureaucracy and its environment that might be responsible for the differential innovativeness of states. For such guidance it is only logical to turn to the literature on innovation within complex organizations. Unfortunately, even with the aid of that literature, the tasks of identifying potentially relevant dimensions and explicating the precise manner in which they are anticipated to affect innovativeness is anything but straightforward. This is true because no well-integrated, monolithic theory of innovation exists—only a loosely related set of widely varying perspectives that must be sifted in order to determine the ways they complement or contradict each other, where different terms are used to speak of similar concepts, and when similar language is used to talk about very disparate ideas.

The next three chapters are organized on the basis of the source of the determinants analyzed. Chapter 3 deals with the impact of the general political, social, and economic ecology of the state. Chapter 4 discusses the effect of variations in the task environment of the state agency responsible for administering juvenile corrections. And Chapter 5 looks at the characteristics of the agency and its top administrator and how they affect innovativeness. The final chapter (6) contains the substantive, theoretical, and methodological conclusions.

**Bureaucracy, Innovation,
and Public Policy**

1

Research into the Determinants of State Policy Outputs

The recent decade witnessed the emergence of comparative policy research[a] as the principal vehicle for the development of a "positive theory" of public policy formation, or a theory that is

. . . in principle independent of any particular ethical position or normative judgements. Its task is to provide a system of generalizations that can be used to make correct predictions about the consequences of any change in circumstances [Friedman, 1953:4].

The type of analysis employed to this end, with its emphasis on the systematic and comparative study of policy outputs and their determinants, constitutes a significant departure from both the exploration of the operation of governmental structures that characterized traditional political science and the normative and nonempirical concerns of welfare economics.

Past studies in the broad area of public policy primarily focused their attention on the structure of governmental institutions and their operations. This emphasis has led to the fashionable and somewhat uncharitable assertion that the authors of these studies suffered from a myopia induced by the a priori assumption that "the products of the political system and/or the rate at which they are delivered are determined in large part by the way in which they are produced and that this in turn is shaped by the structure and composition of political institutions" [Falcone and Whittington, 1972:1]. However, it would be a mistake to attribute the great attention these studies gave governmental institutions to such a naive assumption. The importance of structural variables (i.e., characteristics of these institutions) was continually demonstrated by the methodology employed—the case study—and its tendency to concentrate on "proximate causes."

Case studies have traditionally been concerned with the behavior of "actors" in what often amounts to a narrowly defined closed system. A researcher seeking to understand governmental expenditures elects to do a case study of a legislature since one of its principal functions is to allocate public funds. The selected legislature is exhaustively described and analyzed in terms of how members are elected, as well as their goals, the norms of the legislature, and its relationship with the executive and

---

[a]Alternately termed determinants research.

1

interest groups. Unfortunately, the larger societal forces that constrain and motivate the behavior of the legislators (by determining the nature and definition of problems and the resources available to deal with them) are frequently difficult or impossible to detect when doing a single case study. This limitation results in a natural bias towards explaining the nature of a decision solely in terms of aspects of the legislature similar to those enumerated above, without reference to the characteristics of the larger system (or "antecedent variables") that may, in fact, determine all the important parameters of the output. In a sense, the researcher has been forced to postulate—on the basis of no evidence—that the legislature can be analyzed as part of a "decomposable" or "nearly decomposable" system [Simon, 1969:99–102].

The most straightforward way to identify these antecedent variables is through comparative research or a time-series analysis. Most of the determinants research with which we will be concerned, whether cross-sectional or longitudinal, has been comparative in nature. This research (across cities, states, and nations) has formed the basis of what Jacob and Vines [1971:558] derisively term "the new orthodoxy": the assertion that political structures and processes possess relatively little explanatory power over outputs when compared with the general socioeconomic characteristics of the political system in question.

Past Research

In 1952 Solomon Fabricant published the first quantitative analysis of the determinants of public policy outputs across the states. By using correlation techniques he was able to account for 72 percent of the interstate variation in total state and local per capita expenditures for the year 1942. His independent variables consisted of three socioeconomic characteristics: per capita income, urbanization, and population density[b] [Fabricant, 1952:123]. When expenditures were broken down by functional area (e.g., highways, education), the three variables continued to explain from 29 to 85 percent of the interstate variance.[c] Fabricant [1952:130] concluded that, overall, income was by far the principal determinant, although urbanization appeared to be the most important factor in the areas of fire prevention, sanitation, and welfare. His only comment on the greater importance of urbanization in those areas was that it seemed "reasonable." Similarly, he declined to elaborate on the widely varying aggregate

---

[b]The terms *ecological* and *environmental* are used interchangeably with *socioeconomic* to describe such variables.

[c]The categories still include both state and local expenditures.

explanatory power of his three variables. As will become apparent, this work strongly resembles subsequent research in terms of the kinds of independent and dependent variables examined, the methodological techniques employed, and the reluctance to explore the possible implications of the findings.

Extensions of Fabricant's work appeared in a series of articles in the *National Tax Journal* during the early sixties [Fisher, 1961, 1964; Sacks and Harris, 1964; Bahl and Saunders, 1965; Davis and Haines, 1966]. New explanatory variables were added (overwhelmingly socioeconomic in character), more emphasis was placed on isolating various categories of expenditures, and some initial attention was directed to the determinants of changes in expenditure levels. It was discovered that the explanatory power of the three independent variables utilized by Fabricant decreased over time to account for only 50 percent of the variance in total per capita expenditures in 1957 [Fisher, 1961:352]. Consistent with Fabricant's findings, it became increasingly apparent that environmental variables had a differential impact across expenditure categories, although once again no one attempted to explore why this was the case. In particular, no one offered an explanation as to why welfare expenditures were proving to be increasingly inexplicable in terms of socioeconomic variables [Fisher, 1961:352; Bahl and Saunders, 1965:53].

Other characteristics that would come to form the popular stereotype of determinants research began to emerge during this period. For the most part, the work was quite atheoretical, with the selection of explanatory variables based primarily on considerations of expediency. Whatever might work was included; whatever did work was reported. The goal of this early work was unembarrassingly that of prediction. No model of the policy-making process guided research, and substantive and theoretical considerations rarely appeared as anything other than awkward appendages to numerous tables. This helps to explain how researchers were able to observe the decreasing explanatory power of Fabricant's variables without being led to the tentative conclusion that some kind of "threshold" effect might be occurring—that is, perhaps after a certain level of industrialization or urbanization has been reached, incremental increases in these characteristics are simply not that important in terms of policy outputs.

The goals of increasing and partitioning the percentage of explained variance (R^2) were pursued with such single-mindedness that significant methodological problems and their implications were often overlooked. Conclusions about the relative importance of explanatory variables were made despite extensive multicollinearity (e.g., between urbanization and population density) and were based on statistical techniques whose causal assumptions and inferential limitations were largely unnoticed.

Doubtless a large part of the explanation for the atheoretical nature of this early work stems from the fact that it was conducted by a few economists who had no interest in constructing a theory of policy making or formulating strategies of social change. Their research was largely ignored by political scientists who, at the time, often lacked the necessary technical sophistication to deal with it and possessed the previously mentioned bias toward process characteristics. At the time, most political scientists had relatively little interest in policy outputs and outcomes and virtually none in the significance of environmental inputs. The mutual isolation of the two disciplines ended with publication in 1963 of an important article by Dawson and Robinson.

In "Interparty Competition, Economic Variables, and Welfare Policies in the American States," Dawson and Robinson set out to test the Key-Lockard hypothesis that increased interparty competition leads to a higher level of welfare expenditures. By adopting a simple systems model in which characteristics of the formal policy-making process function as intervening variables between inputs (socioeconomic characteristics) and policy outputs, the authors sought to discover whether interparty competition had an independent effect on welfare expenditures after socioeconomic characteristics were controlled by means of partial correlations. They concluded that although the level of party competition was related to welfare expenditures, its independent effect was not substantial and the apparent relationship was largely spurious. Welfare expenditures seemed to be more a function of environmental factors, especially per capita income [Dawson and Robinson, 1963:289].[d]

Among the article's several significant contributions to state policy analysis, two related ones are especially noteworthy. First, the article was motivated by theoretical considerations. An important and widely held hypothesis was tested, and the implications of the negative findings were substantial, thereby raising "serious doubts about the relevance of many variables that most political scientists had valued for their ability to explain public policy" [Hofferbert, 1972:6]. Questions such as "Does politics matter?" and "Does environmental determinism exist?" began to be asked for the first time, although usually in a tone of hostile facetiousness. Secondly, their investigation was guided by a model (albeit a crude one) of the policy-making process. From this point forward, despite

---

[d]These results seem to partially contradict earlier work that showed that only a relatively small portion (negligible in one case) of the variance in welfare expenditures could be explained in terms of socioeconomic variables. This apparent paradox can be resolved if we observe that previous studies were measuring per capita welfare expenditures (welfare expenditures divided by state population)—a measurement of total state effort—while Dawson and Robinson measured levels of service delivery (e.g., average unemployment payment per recipient).

extremely slow progress and occasional relapses, researchers would attempt to develop and refine that model rather than engage in the undirected statistical manipulation of any variables at hand.

With Dye's *Politics, Economics, and the Public: Policy Outcomes in the United States* [1966], quantitative policy analysis was firmly established in the mainstream of political science, and the "new orthodoxy" gathered considerable momentum. Employing a theoretical framework similar to that of Dawson and Robinson, Dye used correlation techniques to analyze the relationship between four socioeconomic and four political variables, and fifty-four easily quantifiable policy outputs, primarily expenditure levels.[e] Consistent with the findings of Dawson and Robinson, Dye [1966:293] concludes:

Economic development shapes both political systems and policy outcomes, and most of the association that occurs between system characteristics and policy outcomes can be attributed to the influence of economic development. Differences in the policy choices of states with different types of political systems turn out to be largely a product of differing socioeconomic levels rather than a direct product of political variables. Levels of urbanization, industrialization, income, and education appear to be more influential in shaping policy outcomes than political system characteristics.

Typical of Dye's analysis is his investigation of the effect of malapportionment on welfare policy. The reasoning behind an expectation that there should be a relationship between the two is simple: Malapportionment usually overrepresents rural and historically conservative constituencies in state legislatures, while certain categories of welfare expenditures (e.g., unemployment compensation) principally affect those who live in urban areas. Therefore we would anticipate that the liberality of a state legislature on welfare matters would decline as the degree of malapportionment increases. However, expectations of an independent relationship were not fulfilled:

When the effects of economic development are controlled, these relationships between urban underrepresentation and welfare outcomes disappear. Whatever association there is between urban underrepresentation and welfare policy it is clearly a product of the fact that levels of economic development influence both welfare policy and urban underrepresentation . . . . reapportionment, in and of itself, is not likely to bring about a noticeable liberalization of welfare policy [Dye, 1966:148].

Dye's work has been the target of considerable criticism, a large

---

[e]The socioeconomic variables were urbanization, industrialization, per capita income, and education. The political variables were partisanship, party competition, voter turnout, and degree of malapportionment.

portion of which has been somewhat cavalier. While it is true that his results are somewhat more ambiguous than he would have us believe (e.g., in a number of areas political variables seem to have an independent effect worthy of some attention) and that his research suffers from several theoretical and methodological shortcomings, his work is not blindly quantitative nor does he contend to have proven conclusively that politics has no effect on outputs (or outcomes, in Dye's terminology). His contribution, and it was a major one, consisted of pointing out that in many categories of public policy, socioeconomic variables appear to be more powerful determinants of state-local expenditures than the political factors continually emphasized in the political science literature. Yet despite the fact that environmental factors had been shown to be the more important, they still left an average of almost two-thirds of the variation in outputs unexplained [Hofferbert, 1972:39]. Although the impact of a few prominent political variables often appeared to be insignificant, environmental determinism had not yet arrived.

The comparative study of state policy determinants improved somewhat in terms of theoretical and methodological sophistication after Dye's book was published. The drawbacks of aggregating state and local expenditures and then trying to explain them only in terms of state-level political variables soon became apparent, and this approach was subsequently abandoned [Morss, 1966; Sharkansky, 1967]. Similarly, the desirability of disaggregating large categories of expenditures on theoretical grounds was also recognized. This led to interesting findings such as the fact that environmental variables had differential effects on various educational outputs, such as teacher salaries and per pupil expenditures [Sharkansky, 1967]. Imaginative dependent variables were also created, which cut across conventional categories (e.g., Fry and Winters's [1970] redistribution index) and which occasionally measured outputs in terms other than expenditures (e.g., Walker's [1969] index of innovativeness).

New structural variables were employed, such as the tenure of the governor and his degree of control over the budget [Schlesinger, 1965] and the percentage of state employees covered by civil service [Fry and Winters, 1970]. In addition, attention was paid to the historical development of the states and regions as possible sources of variations in outputs [Sharkansky, 1968].

Simultaneous refinements in the selection of potentially significant structural variables and in the techniques of analysis have combined to erode the glib simplicity of the new orthodoxy. For example, Fry and Winters [1970] drew variables from several different dimensions (socioeconomic composition, mass political behavior, governmental institutions, and elite behavior) in order to explore the determinants of redistribution—a cleverly constructed dependent variable less sensitive to total amounts of expenditures than to different patterns of distribution.

They discovered that political variables were considerably *more* powerful predictors of interstate variations in redistribution than were socioeconomic variables, and they concluded that politics may play a dominant role "in the allocation of the burdens and benefits of public policies" [Fry and Winters, 1970:522]. Other, even more recent, research [Falcone and Whittington, 1972; Booms and Halldorson, 1973; LeMay, 1973; Gray and Wanat, 1974] has done much to raise the level of discourse in the field.

It is extremely difficult to make confident generalizations about the broader implications of determinants research. Like most social science research, "it is easier to see how little we have accomplished and to list the reasons why we have been able to do so little than to recognize what, in fact, we have been accomplishing" [Fried, 1973:16].

The accepted technique for evaluating the implications of the comparative policy analysis literature appears to consist of making a series of provocative generalizations about the marginality of politics, and then qualifying them in such a way that the reader is left with little idea of the significance of the research. For instance, in evaluating the findings of research into the determinants of urban policies, Fried [1973:73] states:

The impact of only a few political variables has been tested in relatively few contexts, using relatively few and possibly unreliable and invalid indicators for both political variables and for the policy outcomes which they allegedly fail to influence. Part of the weakness of political variables may be only apparent. The impact of political variables may be hidden by the use of extremely equivocal indicators.

Although these sorts of qualifications are appropriate in the sense that they are based on valid criticisms, they have a tendency to preempt further speculation about the implications for policy theory. This is unfortunate because, notwithstanding their limitations, determinants studies do seem to be telling us something of interest.

Minimally, there would seem to be at least four conclusions that might be drawn:

1. The determinants of policy outputs vary *within* an area (e.g., education) just as, previously, they were seen to vary *between* policy areas (e.g., highways versus welfare). As Sharkansky and Hofferbert [1969:878] state: "There is no simple answer to the question: 'Is it politics or economics that has the greatest impact on public policy?' The answer varies with the dimensions of each phenomenon that are at issue." This discovery should have prompted speculation that the traditional categorization of outputs by service area (e.g., health, education) may be dysfunctional to the advancement of theory building and that we should seek other bases for classifying outputs. Unfortunately this has not been the case.

2. Despite their differential effect across various policy outputs, socioeconomic variables are important determinants of public policy and must be recognized as such. This recognition must consist of more than a perfunctory admission of the obvious and must be thoughtfully investigated through the use of causal models and sensitively integrated into policy recommendations and social change strategies. There is little doubt that the environment (even as narrowly defined in terms of socioeconomic variables) is a principal source of constraints on the alternatives available to decisionmakers, although a considerable number of questions remain to be asked about the exact manner in which the environment affects outputs (i.e., the nature of the linkages between the environment and policy outputs) and the time spans in which these constraints are operative (i.e., short run versus long run).[f]

3. Although political variables have regained some of the luster they lost as a result of earlier work in the field, it is clear that much of the a priori speculation regarding the extent and direction of their impact on policy outputs is in need of revision. There is now considerable evidence that suggests that political variables, at least as they are usually conceived, do not have a consistently significant effect on an enormous number of outputs. Widely held beliefs about the effects of malapportionment, partisan control, and other political variables, while not always shown to have been entirely in error, are certainly revealed to be overly simplistic, and a number of traditional assumptions about the policy-making process now appear naive at best. As we have seen, this is an integral part of the supposedly heretical and glib "new orthodoxy," but glib or not, the evidence warrants serious consideration.

Falcone and Whittington operationalized dozens of political variables in a study of the determinants of output change in Canada after lamenting (like Fried) the inadequacy of the indicators of the political process that had been used and the "risky generalizations" about the irrelevance of politics that have emerged [Falcone and Whittington, 1972:27]. The result?

What is striking is the virtual absence of independent or additive relationships between political variables and output measures. . . . the central unifying conclusion emerging from our preliminary study is that the proverbial Alpha Centaurian, if he had all the information on Canadian politics we have been able to quantify, would know no more about output change in Canada than if he knew only the information we have in crude form on socioeconomic change [Falcone and Whittington, 1972:50].

4. There is still a considerable amount of variation left unexplained by the environmental, political, and the few organizational variables that

---

[f]For enlightening discussions on the significance of short-run versus long-run constraints see Simon and Ando [1961] and Fisher and Ando [1962].

have been used up to this point. This is especially true in output categories that are not as closely tied to expenditures (e.g., teacher preparation as opposed to per pupil expenditures).

General Criticisms and Possible Explanations

Such relatively modest conclusions should indicate that determinants research has been less than successful in its attempt to fashion a powerful positive theory of policy formation. Further evidence of this can readily be found in (1) the "instability" of research findings whereby the explanatory power of many variables (particularly structural or process ones) varies widely across output categories, states, and time; (2) the large amount of output variation left unexplained; and (3) the negligible prescriptive contribution that determinants research has made to policy formation.

1. *Instability*: Although the cumulative results of a number of studies occasionally permit us to make tentative generalizations about the effect of certain broad categories of variables on specific types of policy outputs (e.g., socioeconomic variables seem to be important determinants of aggregate expenditures across the states), the instability of findings that describe the impact of individual system characteristics across a number of policy areas is somewhat disconcerting. A given variable or set of variables will be a major determinant of per pupil expenditures but not of teacher credentials, of AFDC expenditures but not of Aid to the Blind. Legislative professionalism will be seen to explain 25 percent of the variance in one output but less than two percent in another [LeMay, 1973]. Three variables will account for 72 percent of the variance in an output category in one year and only 50 percent in the same category a decade later [Fisher, 1961:352].

2. *Unexplained variance*: While their success in achieving a high degree of variance explained has not been appreciably less than that of researchers in most other areas of social science, there is considerable room for improvement. Hofferbert [1973:39] is fond of pointing out that despite the furor brought on by Dye's early work [1966] over the possibility of environmental determinism, an averge of two-thirds of the variance in fifty-four output categories could *not* be accounted for by socioeconomic variables. Recent studies have often achieved higher R^2s, but they have rarely exceeded .4 or .5 and have frequently been much lower, *especially* when nonexpenditure output measures have been employed. The impact of individual variables has usually been very small.

3. *Prescriptive sterility*: The characteristics described above would not lead one to expect determinants research to be of great utility for those responsible for policy making and those interested in fostering

social change. Such pessimism has been amply justified over the years, but this deficiency has not been merely an artifact of empirical findings; it has also been the result of intent (or the lack of it). Just as theoretical concerns were absent from early research in the field, prescriptive concerns have rarely been evident. It is common to attribute this defect of most comparative state policy studies to a regrettable but understandable preoccupation with the development of macrotheory. Yet one wonders whether macrotheory truly demands it.

There are two possible explanations for the deficiencies described above that have not received the emphasis they deserve in the numerous and elaborate critiques of comparative policy analysis. The first concerns the nature of the explanatory or independent variables included in determinants studies, and the second, the manner in which these variables are hypothesized to relate to policy outputs.

There is an extensive and well-developed body of theoretical and case study material [e.g., Rourke, 1969; Lowi, 1969; Halperin, 1974] that emphasizes the fact that an ever-increasing proportion of policy decisions are being made by bureaucracies. Elected officials, particularly legislators, frequently do not possess the time, information, or expertise required to deal with complex social, economic, or scientific issues. Furthermore, many policy decisions must be made that have no appreciable "political payoff" for elected officials, either because their constituents (and contributors) are indifferent to the outcome, or because they risk alienating a significant portion of their constituencies regardless of which alternative they select and therefore would rather avoid responsibility for the decision.[g] These factors, according to popular wisdom, have combined to erode any remnant of the rigid Wilsonian distinction between policy making and administration. They have created a situation in which bureaucracies structure the agendas and define the alternatives for elected officials, and are permitted great autonomy in administrative decision making. Whether such delegation of authority to bureaucracies has become pathological, as Lowi [1969] argues, or not, there appears to be no question that for public bureaucracies the task of policy making has assumed parity with that of policy implementation.

If we accept the hypothesis that many key policy decisions are now made by bureaucrats rather than by legislators or other elected officials, then the finding of the comparative state literature that political variables often fail to have a significant independent impact on policy outputs should come as no surprise. In fact, that hypothesis should have led us to expect precisely what determinants studies have found.

Yet despite all of the work done during the past twenty years on the

---

[g]This is equivalent to saying that the constituency exchange values are low for these decisions [Salisbury and Heinz, 1970].

increasing power of the bureaucracy, bureaucratic or organizational variables[h] are consistently underrepresented in determinants research, while such factors as party competition and voter turnout are tossed into almost every analysis regardless of theoretical relevance. The reasons for the omission of these variables can largely be attributed to problems of cost (field research is often needed to secure such data), the traditionally legislative bias of political scientists, and the researcher's frequent lack of familiarity with the problem area under analysis. Except in the field of education, researchers have possessed very little substantive knowledge about a particular policy area. However, part of the blame can also be placed on the shoulders of organizational theorists and others who, while stressing the importance of the bureaucracy, seem reluctant to identify the dimensions of the bureaucracy and bureaucratic behavior that are responsible for variations in policy outputs. Is the degree of centralization important? Professionalization? Complexity? Formalization? Should a policy researcher be interested in examining the impact of the bureaucracy and its environment, it is commonly the case that no obvious source of guidance is available.

The problem with the resultant situation (i.e., the omission of bureaucratic variables) is not only that the goal of high explanatory power is left unattained because relevant variables have been unknowingly excluded but that the resultant model is theoretically and prescriptively sterile. Such sterility arises from the fact that no attempt is made to systematically specify the "linkages" between socioeconomic variables and policy outputs. Once again we see the consequences of the field's early emphasis on prediction rather than explanation, on parameters instead of process. If this field is to progress, such a black-box approach, which precludes serious causal modeling and almost encourages making inferences on the basis of spurious relationships, can no longer be acceptable.

Recognizing the necessity of attempting to specify the linkages among variables also leads to speculation about the nature of those linkages. In what manner do variables interrelate and what is the functional form of their statistical relationships? Are there conditions under which we might expect urbanization or bureaucratic centralization to have a greater or lesser effect on outputs? Does party competition have the same effect in states where the two parties are ideologically similar as it does in states where they are far apart? Such considerations inevitably raise doubts about the appropriateness of the almost exclusive utilization of additive models in determinants research.[i]

---

[h]Such variables are broadly defined here to include aspects of "bureaucratic politics" and certain elite characteristics as well as conventional bureaucratic variables.

[i]The only exceptions known to the author are Strouse and Williams [1972], Broach [1973], and Gray and Wanat [1974].

The argument that interactive models could profitably be used in terms of increasing the proportion of variance explained, gaining insight into the nature of the policy process, and accounting for the instability of research findings appears fairly convincing. Recall the instance mentioned previously when researchers discovered that the explanatory power of Fabricant's three socioeconomic variables declined from 72 percent in 1942 to 50 percent in 1957 [Fisher, 1961:352]. The sort of threshold effect already discussed provides one possible explanation for this phenomenon and is a special case of interaction. Along the same lines, there is reason to believe that the influence of political variables on policy outputs is affected by a nation's or state's level of socioeconomic development [Peters, 1972]. Perhaps only at high levels of development do political or bureaucratic variables assume any importance at all (another threshold hypothesis), or it may be that the impact of these variables increases in direct proportion to increases in development. Hypotheses like these become quite plausible if one looks upon many political and bureaucratic variables (e.g., partisanship, professionalism) as providing the motivation to alter the present level of policy outputs, and economic variables as supplying the requisite resources [Mohr, 1969]. High motivation alone would be insufficient to ensure a high output level, and our model could no longer postulate that the impact of political and bureaucratic variables is independent of levels on economic variables— that these variables relate to outputs in an additive fashion.

Frequently researchers have proceeded with the use of additive regression equations when theoretical considerations made their use questionable. For example, are we right in anticipating that legislative professionalism will have the same impact in states that are legislatively dominated (e.g., Arizona) as it does in states where policy initiation is historically the province of the governor (e.g., New York)? If we are not, then the coefficient produced by an additive model will be an unenlightening "average" that reveals little about the real "contingent" impact of the variable. Like legislative professionalism, the impact of many of the characteristics commonly included in determinants studies may be contingent on one or more other variables.

Moreover, if we expand the usual definition of determinant to include characteristics of the choice situation,[j] interactive models can potentially permit us to account for the sharp variations in findings across studies that

---

[j]Characteristics of the choice situation describe the *relationship* between a given governmental unit and a given output as opposed to a characteristic of the governmental unit that can be measured independently from any output attribute. Variables such as "need" and "output uncertainty" fall into this first category since they require a referent outside the governmental unit (i.e., need for ———, or uncertainty about ——— output). See Downs and Mohr [1975].

have dealt with different policy outputs. Certainly it only seems reasonable to anticipate that the impact of many variables may alter as we move from one output to another. The effect of per capita income may depend on the price tag attached to increments of an output. Similarly, the impact of legislative characteristics may depend on the constituency exchange values attached to alternatives.

The tasks of exploring the impact of characteristics of bureaucracies and their environments and intelligently searching for the interaction among such variables would, of course, be greatly facilitated if we knew which characteristics to measure and what patterns of interaction could be expected to exist. The traditional political science literature offers virtually no help here, but there is a well-developed literature on the determinants of innovation in complex organizations, to which we now turn.

2

Public Policy and Innovation Theory

Policy as Innovation

The application of research into the determinants of innovation in organizations to the study of public policy formation has a strong intuitive appeal. Many of the most important and visible policy decisions at all levels of government involve new programs or qualitative departures from traditional operations, and these decisions are increasingly being made in a bureaucratic context. In fact, the task of innovating has become an integral part of the bureaucratic mandate.

While an understanding of the process and determinants of bureaucratic innovation may not help us to explain aggregate output data such as expenditure levels, it should aid us in accounting for variations in such things as the adoption and implementation of poverty programs or state licensing practices for nursing homes.

The amount and breadth of research on the topic of innovation would seem capable of providing considerable direction for a study of public sector policy innovation and the factors surrounding it. Rogers and Shoemaker include a bibliography of some 1,500 items in their 1971 book, and by now, assuming a constant growth rate, there are probably more than 2,500. The range of different academic perspectives represented is equally impressive. Rogers and Shoemaker [1971:387–88] enumerate eighteen research traditions, from anthropology to speech. Not surprisingly, such diversity is also indicat ve of considerable incompatibility with respect to the innovations considered and their measurement, the explanatory variables that are included, and the research aims of the authors. This should serve to temper our optimism, as should the fact that in social science, empirical richness is rarely accompanied by theoretical richness.

This chapter seeks to accomplish a variety of foundation-laying tasks for what follows. First, we will examine two of the principal, and by far the most relevant, traditions in innovation research. The goals of this discussion are to determine their potential contributions to, and limitations for, an investigation of public policy innovation and then begin to look at how their key concepts might be translated for inclusion in a comparative study of policy-making across the states. The goodness of fit between the two traditions and research into the determinants of state policy innovation will be described at some length. Next, we will survey three studies by political scientists who have attempted to apply innovation theory to public policy. This is followed by a detailed description of the correctional innovation of deinstitutionalization and its relationship with the types of innovations normally found in the literature. Last, some of the broad research goals of the next three chapters are summarized in terms of questions suggested by the application of the various traditions to the specific problem of explaining interstate variation in deinstitutionalization rates.

The Sociological Approach

There are at least two reasons for anticipating that the research on innovation conducted by sociologists and a small number of political scientists who are solidly in the same tradition should be directly applicable to the study of policy innovation. First, the majority of these studies have been carried out in formal organizations, many of which are in the public sector. Second, they have frequently dealt with programmatic innovations as well as technological ones.

Table 2–1 contains a list of those characteristics of organizations that have, with some regularity, been found to be associated (not necessarily

Table 2–1
Organizational Attributes Associated with Innovativeness

Complexity
Heterogeneity
Formalization
Impersonal relations
Job satisfaction
Organic structure
Rate of environmental change
Contact with information sources
Slack/resources
Presence of crisis
Specialization
Conflict-reducing mechanism
Participative decision making

Sources: Rogers and Shoemaker [1971] and Zaltman et al. [1973].

positively) with the adoption of innovation. This list is noteworthy in a number of respects. Perhaps most evident is the preponderance of internal and/or structural characteristics (formalization, complexity, etc.), and it would be no exaggeration to say that structural variables have dominated innovation research in the sociological tradition almost from the beginning.[a] This domination can probably be attributed to the profound

---

[a]See, for instance, Burns and Stalker [1961] and Hage and Aiken [1967].

impact of Max Weber on all aspects of organization theory and to the desire of researchers to discover manipulatable attributes of organizations that foster the adoption of *any* given innovation. The two are closely related and indicative of a very instrumental view of organizations. Weber viewed bureaucracy as the most efficient tool that can exist for large-scale administration, and the implicit goal of most sociologically oriented innovation research is to design the organization that will be the most conducive to the adoption of innovations—one that is efficient in the sense of offering the least resistance to adoption. This emphasis on organizational design and the identification of key structural attributes has strongly influenced the evolution of sociological research on innovation in three major and interconnected ways.

First, sociological research on the determinants of innovativeness has been predominantly and rather disproportionately concerned with those factors that *facilitate* adoption as opposed to those characteristics that *motivate* it. While attention to the first category of variables is obviously in order, when it takes place at the expense of exploring motivational variables, we are left with a severely truncated model. It is difficult to be completely satisfied with a study that, by the choice of variables for inclusion in the analysis, appears to be arguing that organizations adopt innovations primarily because they can do so effortlessly. We need to explore variation in the *benefits* that organizations gain from adoption as well as the structural variables that make adoption *easier,* unless we are willing to make the improbable assumption that the benefits are always the same for every organization and thus can be disregarded.

Researchers and theorists in the sociological tradition occasionally seek to redress this lopsidedness by acknowledging the importance of "performance gaps" [Zaltman et al., 1973:2] and "need" [Zaltman et al., 1973:118]. However, such variables are rarely included as independent variables in models used to predict or explain innovativeness; nor, for that matter, has there ever been any empirical attempt to identify (a) what it is that causes variations in need or the size of performance gaps, (b) the nature of the interaction between structure and need, or (c) the relative impact of each in leading an organization to adopt an innovation. Consistent with this, the sociological tradition has been very slow in acquiring an understanding of the microincentives or decision rules operative in the process of innovation.

Second, the emphasis on organizational design has encouraged a fundamental decomposition and separation of characteristics of the organization from those of the innovation, which reinforces the concentration on facilitating factors. The attempt to formulate universally applicable principles for fostering a high degree of general innovativeness in organizations encourages the researcher to avoid organizational variables that are *innovation specific* in the sense that the organization could not receive a score on the variable until a particular innovation has been specified.[b] Motivational variables appear, at least at first glance, much more likely to be innovation specific than do structural variables, which seem to be attributes of the organization that are independent of any particular innovation. Certainly it is true that to attempt to determine an organization's level of need for innovations "in general" would be a theoretical and methodological nightmare. Obviously the extent to which organizations need innovations varies from innovation to innovation. Unlike motivational variables, facilitating factors and structural characteristics appear to avoid this problem and therefore to hold the key to a general theory of innovativeness.

Surely an organization is either more or less specialized, formalized, complex, or participative regardless of the innovation being studied. But is this really true? Deeper analysis indicates that even structural characteristics, if they are to be rigorously defined and their suspected impact carefully thought through, are most meaningful only when tied to a specific decision or a category of decisions, for as the nature of the decision changes (here the decision to adopt a given innovation), structure can also "change." Not even in the most formalized and rigid hierarchy is every decision made by the same process or individual; almost invariably an organization is more centralized with respect to some decisions than others. For a particular organization, centralization, formalization, the ability of mechanisms to reduce conflict, and so forth can vary from decision to decision, from innovation to innovation, in a manner quite similar to that of need. The variation may not be as great, but it certainly exists and could become quite significant when we are attempting to explain the adoption of a specific innovation. Once it is acknowledged that what is needed is to analytically characterize the decision-making context and process of adoption (the choice setting and the process of choice) rather than the identification of fundamental, independent, and timeless characteristics of the organization, variables other than structural ones will begin to find their way into analyses.

The questionable nature of the practice of defining and scoring properties of the organization independently of the innovation or set of innovations under consideration becomes clearer when we look at the opposite practice. Table 2–2 replicates a table found in Zaltman et al. [1973:47] that summarizes the major attributes of innovations that determine their adoption.

Table 2–2 indicates that a number of the motivational variables found absent from the first list are not ignored entirely by the sociological tradition but instead are considered to be characteristics of the innova-

---

[b]Examples of such variables are "need" and "expected return on investment."

Table 2–2
Attributes of Innovations that Determine Adoptability

Financial cost	Demonstrability
Social cost	Terminality
Returns to investment	Reversibility
Efficiency	Divisibility
Risk and uncertainty	Degree of commitment
Communicability	Impact on interpersonal relationships
Clarity of results	Publicness
Compatibility	Number of gatekeepers
Pervasiveness	Susceptibility to successions modification
Complexity	Gateway capacity
Perceived relative advantages	

tion. But it is clear that the score we assign an innovation on "returns to investment" or "perceived relative advantage" cannot be determined until we look at the set of organizations who are the potential adopters. For any given innovation, different organizations will variously perceive the relative advantage and returns it offers them.[c] Somehow these variables and *their* determinants must be carefully specified and integrated into any model that would seek to explain why a policy like deinstitutionalization was adopted at different times or to different extents by the organizations or states involved.

Still a third effect of the sociologists' organizational design perspective has been to focus almost all attention on internal characteristics of the organization while neglecting the role of organizational environments in determining the adoption of innovations.[d] Table 2–1 contains only two environmental variables (the rate of change, and the frequency of contact with the environment), and they are not generally represented in the literature any more adequately than this indicates. The sources of this neglect are intimately related to the former two points. An organization's environment is difficult to conceive of in terms of manipulatable variables or facilitating factors, although organizations can and do manipulate their environments. In addition, it is problematic to score organizations on environmental dimensions while maintaining the schism between characteristics of the environment and those of the innovation. It would probably be no exaggeration to say that across the universe of organizational decisions, environments are never absolutely stable in their composition or in the impact of their elements. This fact is probably particularly true in the public sector. As the issue area changes, as we move from one policy

---

[c]The variation is not only a result of perception; organizations will, in fact, achieve different levels of profit from the same innovation.

[d]Contributing to this neglect has been the fact that it is only recently that organization theory as a discipline has begun to exhibit any interest in organizational environments.

innovation to another, the bureaucracy finds itself dealing with different environmental elements, priorities, and coalitions.

From the point of view of trying to understand why policy innovation takes place, the literature's lack of attention to organizational and bureaucratic environments severely limits its relevance. It is hard to imagine, for example, trying to explain the adoption of open-housing ordinances among cities on the basis of a set of variables that includes the power of the mayor and city council, the frequency and duration of council meetings, and the city election process but omits the percentage of blacks, the socioeconomic status of both blacks and whites, and the number, influence, and character of interest groups.

A defender of the approach that concentrates principally on internal characteristics of the organization might argue that this criticism, while true, is insensitive to the limited goals of this research, which seeks only to analyze the impact of a specific set of manipulatable variables. However, this argument is weak on at least two counts. First, even though we might be interested primarily in the impact of structural variables, we would still like to know whether this impact is tied to or independent of other, possibly causally antecedent, variables that are characteristics of the organizational environment. Political scientists engaged in investigating the effect of legislative professionalism and party competition viewed the association between them and expenditures in quite a different light after it was discovered that these two variables were closely tied to per capita income and education, suggesting that the latter rather than the former were really responsible for the increased spending. Second, since Lawrence and Lorsch's [1967] research on the relationship of environment and structure to organizational performance, students of organization theory have increasingly come to believe that the effect of a particular form of structure depends on its congruence with certain aspects of the environment. If this is also true with respect to innovation, then to ignore the environment would be equivalent to ignoring the sorts of interaction effects described in Chapter 1, with the same result of our being left with misleading "average" coefficients.

There is, in addition to the research on organizational innovation, a body of research in the sociological tradition that focuses on the social psychological characteristics of individuals who are innovative. Although these studies do not effectively mitigate the tradition's shortcomings that have been cited (e.g., the absence of environmental variables), their focus on possible sources of individual motivation provides us with some additional directions in selecting variables for a study of policy innovation. Table 2–3 includes a list of some of the attributes commonly found to be related to individual innovation.

Such a list is useful in helping us to identify the characteristics of

Table 2–3
Attributes of Individuals Who Innovate

Educational status	Venturesomeness
Social status	Imaginativeness
Achievement motivation	Sociableness
Undogmatic	Cosmopoliteness
Intelligence	Dominance

Sources: Rogers and Shoemaker [1971, chap. 5] and Loy [1969].

bureaucratic elites that might be relevant to an explanation of policy innovations. For example, it indicates that an analysis of the degree and manner in which the bureaucracy is professionalized would prove useful. It also suggests that any measure of professionalism should involve more than just one variable that measures the average years of education among the staff and ought to include information about the social status, ideologies, and mixes of the represented professions. The applicability of this list to the study of elites is clear, and no more will be said about it here except to observe that acquiring all the necessary information is a formidable task, to say the least.

Before attempting to summarize the potential contribution of the sociological tradition to a study of the determinants of policy innovation, it should be mentioned that there is at least one researcher who has been concerned with motivational variables and the issue of interaction. On the basis of his research into the determinants of innovations in public health departments, Mohr [1969] has constructed a multiplicative model that postulates that the decision to innovate is determined by the interaction of two dimensions: *motivation* and *resources*. This kind of interactive model (i.e., a multiplicative one) possesses several interesting characteristics. Both factors must be present for the innovation to occur—that is, both are necessary and neither is sufficient. At the same time, it is possible for a very high value on one factor to compensate for a rather low value on the other. This attribute provides his model with a richness (in the sense that it makes more statements about what is going on) and realism frequently absent from the sociological tradition. From experience we know that a high level of resources accompanied by no motivation leads to a failure to innovate, and vice versa. The smaller either factor becomes, the more the other must increase disproportionately to result in the same behavior.

Beyond sensitizing us to the importance of motivational and resource variables (which by itself is a nontrivial contribution), there is some question about the usefulness of Mohr's model for other than post hoc analysis. Mohr's "superdimensions" are highly abstract and provide no assistance in deciding in advance which resources and which motivations are relevant for a particular output, which are the most important and why. Weighting and scaling the variables that compose these dimensions will also be difficult. On the positive side, the theory admits empirical verification and seems therefore less likely to yield spurious results, and it offers a very plausible alternative to (and implicit critique of) both the statistical and theoretical models predominantly used in the sociological literature on innovation. The next step would appear to be to refine and disaggregate the two dimensions to the point where they permit us to make conditional statements about the anticipated impact of specific dimensions of organizational structure, environment, etc.

In summary, the sociological tradition of innovation research appears capable of providing us with an occasionally helpful but rather limited analytic superstructure of the sort necessary to support even exploratory research. The tradition contains a vast amount of diffuse empirical research that presents us, if we are willing to ferret them out, with a potpourri of potentially significant variables that have not yet found their way into the determinants tradition reviewed in Chapter 1. Drawing the attention of students of public policy to these variables is, by itself, a significant contribution. However, we have also seen that large categories of determinants (e.g., motivational and environmental) have been systematically overlooked. Ironically, with very few exceptions, the sociological tradition suffers from many of the same deficiencies as were observed in connection with the literature on policy determinants. Only Mohr has methodically probed his data for interaction between explanatory variables, and even in the literature's nonempirical theoretical component *conditional* statements about the impact of a variable on the innovativeness of an organization are exceedingly rare.[e]

In addition, the sociological tradition of innovation research has, like research into policy determinants, suffered from a similar overemphasis on exclusively empirical explorations of the determinants of innovativeness at the expense of conducting the necessary dialogue between data and theory, and the application of more formal logical analysis. This is probably at least partially responsible for its failure to deal with the issue of interaction, the awkward separation of characteristics of the innovation from those of the adopter, and the lack of interest in uncovering and specifying the nature of the microprocesses that characterize adoptive behavior.

The Economic Tradition

Unlike sociological research on innovation, from the standpoint of exploring the determinants of public policy innovation, the economic literature

---

[e]For another such attempt in connection with structural variables, see Zaltman et al. [1973:182].

contains relatively little that appears directly relevant. This is not meant to discount the quality of the empirical research done by economists in the field of innovation or the depth of their theoretical work. It is simply that for the most part economists have been concerned with technological rather than program innovation, with the private rather than the public sector, and with research issues only vaguely related to the characteristics of the organization that cause it to be innovative. These factors combine to make it virtually impossible to even attempt to outline a theory of the determinants of public sector innovation solely on the basis of what can be found in the economic literature. On the other hand, one emerges from that literature with a richer understanding of the methodological and theoretical issues that are involved than if one approached the topic exclusively from the perspective of the sociological tradition.

In his excellent critique of the economic and sociological literatures on innovation, Warner [1974:439] points to the complementarity of the two approaches:

The sociological literature is rich in precisely those areas where the economic literature is poor—for example, examination of the personal traits and characteristics of innovators and imitators, and detailed investigation of the communication channels through which information and new knowledge diffuse to potential adopters. Similarly, sociological studies are deficient where economic studies are strong, the former frequently ignoring the influences on diffusion of profit and loss, size of investment and so forth.

Economists have not primarily been concerned with those characteristics of organizations and firms that lead them to adopt innovations. Those few empirical studies by economists that have been concerned with the characteristics of adopters have tended to focus on an extremely limited set of variables: expected return in terms of profit, firm size, age and education of the firm's president; and, more rarely, growth rate, profit trend, and liquidity.[f] This list can be expanded slightly if we wish to include variables that have been treated as characteristics of the innovation but can be expected to vary from one adopter to another. These include the size of the investment required to adopt, risk, uncertainty, and the length of time required before a profit is realized.

There are probably several partial explanations for why economists have focused on such a narrow range of variables in their empirical work on innovation. The most obvious is that they are economists and thus have an ideological (and perhaps genetic) bias toward economic explanations—especially of the behavior of private sector firms operating in competitive markets.

In this context one may say a few words about the impact of "sociological variables": It is my belief that in the long run, and cross-sectionally, these variables tend to

---

[f]See Mansfield [1968], Mansfield et al. [1971], Scherer [1968], and Griliches [1957].

cancel themselves out, leaving the economic variables as the major determinants of the pattern of technological change. . . . With a little ingenuity, I am sure that I can redefine 90 percent of the "sociological variables" as economic variables [Griliches, 1957:522].

Generally economists are much more tolerant (outwardly, at least) of alternative modes of explanation.

Perhaps these variables (i.e., economic ones) are less important than other more elusive and essentially noneconomic variables. The personality attributes, interests, training, and other characteristics of top and middle management may play a very important role in determining how quickly a firm introduces an innovation [Mansfield, 1968b:172].

Yet even Mansfield, the most prolific economist in this particular field, rarely includes such variables in his models, despite the fact that he recognizes their potential importance and even possesses case study and survey evidence to confirm it [Mansfield, 1968:52–53; Mansfield et al., 1971:201]. One is left with the general impression that most economists, not unreasonably, believe that their task is to concentrate on economic variables. And it is only fair to add that this "bias" of economists has been reinforced by success. Griliches, Mansfield, and others have shown that profitability and the size of investment are powerful predictors of adoption and that expected return is a good predictor of innovativeness. Whether this success would continue if we moved from the private to the public sector and from "hardware" innovations to programmatic ones is, of course, questionable.

Another reason for the limited number of adopter characteristics that have been examined by economists has to do with the sorts of research questions with which they usually deal. The majority of their empirical efforts attempt to (a) analyze and describe patterns by which innovations diffuse through organizations and (b) relate these patterns to characteristics of innovations. Obviously, such goals have the effect of either focusing attention on the aggregate behavior of organizations or the characteristics of the innovation as opposed to those of the innovating unit and its environment.

Given their profession's emphasis on the role that markets play in determining the behavior of firms, it is somewhat ironic that economists have not devoted more attention to the impact of environmental characteristics on organizational innovativeness. The only market characteristic treated with any regularity has been the degree of interfirm rivalry (alternately termed the extent of economic concentration or intensity of competition), and even that appears far more frequently in studies of research-and-development behavior than in innovation research.

Apart from the fact that the attention of most studies has been focused on either the aggregate innovative behavior of groups of firms or the characteristics of innovations that determine their adoption, one of the reasons why the impact of environmental characteristics on innovative behavior has been largely ignored by economists is that they have frequently studied the adoptive behavior of homogeneous groups of organizations. Thus, it is often possible for them to assume that all firms in a given analysis are operating in a similar environment—that is, the set of all aircraft or all cement manufacturers are assumed to operate in roughly the same market. If economists found themselves examining the adoption of an innovation such as data processing by a *variety* of different types of firms (e.g., schools, retailers, or manufacturers), more market characteristics would doubtless have appeared as independent variables in their research.

However, perhaps the most important explanation for why economists are able to ignore environmental characteristics while still developing a reasonably satisfactory predictive model is that the impact of these variables in the private sector can be neatly summarized by "expected profits." While this variable may leave something to be desired in providing any significant insight into the process of external command and control, it provides a handy and useful surrogate for a number of unmeasured variables. Unfortunately, as we move from the study of private sector technological innovations to public sector policy and program innovations, we cannot assume that the environments of our units of analysis are similar (i.e., those of states, cities, and so forth), nor is an elegant summary variable such as profit so readily at hand.

If the empirical studies that have been mentioned above made up the entirety of efforts by economists in the field of innovation, the economic tradition might be of no more than passing interest to someone interested in doing research on policy innovation. While it is true that economists, as compared with sociologists, have placed more emphasis on the role of the motivation to innovate—represented by expected profit—it is also true that this variable has no obvious analog in the public sector and that numerous other variables that might be suspected to facilitate or constrain innovative behavior on the part of organizations are usually missing. There are, however, a number of economists, led by Richard Nelson of Yale, who, while not yet engaged in empirical research to any substantial degree, are concerned about matters of interest to students of public sector innovation. The theoretical perspective they have adopted provides some much-needed guidance about the direction in which research and theory building might profitably proceed.

The distinguishing characteristic of this group's approach to the study of innovations is their concern with microbehavior and the incentives and constraints that determine it. Not surprisingly, this approach is characterized by a preoccupation with questions of process and the identification of decision rules as well as a healthy distrust of conventional econometric models composed of macrovariables that can mask more than they reveal. Its resemblance to the Carnegie School's behavioral approach to organization theory is strong and acknowledged.

The goals of specifying decision rules and higher-order "metarules" [Nelson, 1972:42] that guide changes in these rules are quite different from that of identifying deterministic laws and may appear to be incompatible with the survey research methods commonly used in fairly large comparative studies such as this one. The latter is, however, only partially true. While survey methods would provide a cumbersome way to develop a full-fledged process model, they can be used to discover potential candidates for operative decision rules. A high degree of correspondence between the values and priorities of the governor and the policy outputs of a state correctional agency, combined with the response of the director of that agency that he is in frequent contact with the governor and follows his advice on policy matters, can be compelling evidence that we are closing in on that director's decision rules. Decision rules are functions of existing environmental conditions, information flow, the values of policymakers, etc. Survey investigation, while undoubtedly unable to precisely specify these functions, can at least begin to identify the component variables of decision rules. However, discovering what constrains and motivates the satisficing decisionmaker, thereby shaping his decision rules, necessitates gathering a great deal of information about the behavior and perceptions of key decisionmakers. This is something neither the sociological nor the empirical economic traditions have done to any great extent.

Unlike other economists who have studied innovation, those seeking to develop a behavioral model maintain an active interest in key characteristics of the public sector and in exploring their implications for the innovative behavior of the units operating within it:

In most nonmarket sectors (as in market sectors where competition is lax), the firm has a good deal of discretionary power regarding what it is to provide, and the customer may have little direct power to reward or punish performance.

In any case, the motivations of the firms in the sector are not assumed to be monetary profit. Analysis of the operative values of the firms therefore, should be a centerpiece of nonmarket selection. [Nelson and Winter 1975:343].

The quotation above provides a persuasive a priori (as opposed to ex post facto empirical) rationale for gathering data about the personal and professional values of decisionmakers in any study of public sector policy innovation. Certainly there are few areas where the lack of objective evaluative criteria is as conspicuous as it is in the field of corrections.

Whether or not these values should indeed be a "centerpiece" of this research will doubtless depend largely on the role they play in the innovation's "selection environment" (to use Nelson and Winters's Darwinian term), but this is an empirical question that can only be answered after those values have been isolated and included in the analysis. Of course, very few studies have even attempted to simultaneously include an adequately detailed specification of the organization environment and the values of the internal decisionmakers.

Nelson and his colleagues maintain a lively interest in nonmarket environments and their influence on innovation. They emphasize both the potential importance and complexity of these environments, and the arguments they set forth are persuasive. In particular they stress that the formal or informal integration of environmental groups into the decision-making process of the organization by a variety of mechanisms is common in the public sector, and often the range of participants is considerable. This point appears undeniable.

For instance, as will be described in Chapter 4, the environment of a state juvenile corrections bureaucracy consists of courts, the legislature and its staff, the governor and his staff, other state agencies, interest groups, etc. Not all of these groups are necessarily involved in every decision, but frequently decision making in juvenile corrections agencies does take the form of a collective process that includes external groups—not uncommonly by constitutional provision. The fact that so little information is available on the effectiveness of what is being done and the efficiency with which it is being accomplished presents ample opportunity for environmental groups to press claims based on their own self-interest. Both the operative definitions of what is worth doing and how it should be done may emerge from an intimidatingly complex problem in collective decision making. There is every indication that this state of affairs is frequently duplicated throughout many areas of the public sector.

However, while these economists have perceptively described in general terms the complex pattern of demands that comprise the selection environment of a public agency, much work remains to be done in specifying dimensions of that environment useful for empirical research and prescription. What characteristics of the selection environment facilitate or inhibit adoption other than the respective priorities of the actors? Does the integration of demand patterns make any difference? The number of actors? The range of priorities? The frequency, mode, and extent of communication between actors? Questions such as these have barely begun to be articulated.

Overall, the contribution of the economic tradition in innovation research to the study of policy innovation is, like the sociological tradition, less than we might have anticipated and somewhat ambiguous.

Indeed, it consists more in providing a perspective that is different from that of the sociologists and thereby provoking us to consider interesting questions than in suggesting even a tentative model of policy innovation. For example, the importance of "size of investment" in predicting the speed and extent of diffusion suggests that the level of organizational resources would be a good predictor of an organization's innovativeness, but that fact has long been known to sociologists. However, because we are led to postulating the importance of resources *after* recognizing that size of investment is an important attribute of innovations, we become aware of the interaction between the organization and the innovation. This suggests that resources may vary as a predictor of innovativeness *depending* on the cost of the innovation. The level of organizational resources may be a good predictor of the adoption of computerized data processing (an expensive innovation) but an inconsequential predictor of the installation of participative management (a cheap innovation). This places us in the position to generate a testable hypothesis about the conditional role of state resources in determining innovativeness in public policy.

Similarly, the implications for innovation research in nonmarkets of the pivotal role that profitability plays in predicting private sector adoption are significant but not straightforward. Warner [1974:443] seems to advocate the search for an analog to profitability in the public sector, but the probability of finding a satisfactory analog does not appear to be high. In fact, the search, if conducted too literally, may be dysfunctional to theory development. Attempts to substitute "expected value" for expected profit, which at first glance may seem reasonable, are flawed by the aggregate character of the term "value." It possesses the same disadvantages of Mohr's dimension of "motivation." While useful in drawing our attention to a crucial category of variables, its operationalization presents us with too many degrees of freedom: We do not know what variables to include or exclude, and commensurability as we move from one context to another presents incalculable measurement difficulties. There seems to be no doubt that there is no *one* value characteristic that substitutes for expected profit in explaining public sector innovativeness: There are *many*.

In fact, expected value or relative advantage is often indistinguishable from the numerator of the innovation's benefit-cost ratio, which comes closer to being something we would like to explain or predict than an independent variable in a model of the determinants of innovativeness. We need to know what it is about an organization and its environment that makes an innovation beneficial, that makes it valuable. Furthermore, one can argue that in the public arena, the concept of a policy innovation's objective "true worth" can be almost meaningless or, minimally, can ensnarl us in an unwieldy problem in welfare economics. Perhaps, in the last analysis, the discovery by economists that profitability is a powerful determinant of adoption in the private sector can do no more than emphasize the cruciality of uncovering the determinants of "worth" in the public sector.

Political Scientists, Public Policy, and Innovation Research

Several political scientists have attempted to employ some of the techniques and insights of the two traditions of innovation research just described to the study of public policy formation. Walker [1969] looked at the adoption rates of 88 programs ranging from "accountants licensing" to "zoning in cities—enabling legislation" in the fifty states. His findings regarding the determinants of adoption were generally consistent with the determinants literature. Larger, wealthier, and more industrialized states tended to adopt innovations more rapidly than did smaller, less well-developed ones [Walker, 1969:884]. Typically, the independent influence of party competition and executive turnover were not found to be substantial, although apportionment, surprisingly, did have a significant impact on adoption.[g]

Given the results of this correlational analysis, we might conclude that New York, California, and Michigan adopt programs more rapidly than Mississippi, Wyoming, and South Dakota primarily because they are bigger, richer, more urban, more industrial, have more fluidity and turnover in their political systems, and have legislatures which more adequately represent their cities [Walker, 1969:887].

At this point, where most determinants studies conclude, Walker employs innovation theory to explain these statistical relationships. Adopting the Carnegie School approach, which stresses the development of regularized search procedures and decision rules in decision-making behavior, he emphasizes the importance of stable patterns of communication among groups of states and the formation of different reference groups. Knowing the group with which a state identifies and communicates, he argues, will enable us to better predict its behavior, and an overall knowledge of the various reference groups will permit us to better predict the diffusion pattern of a given policy.

To identify these peer groups of states, Walker performed a factor analysis on the fifty states based on their scores for each of the 88 issues.

---

[g]Because reapportionment is itself an innovation, it might be anticipated to occur in "innovative" states. Thus its relationship to other innovations might be spurious rather than causal.

This resulted in five factors that roughly correspond to regions or, in one case, to a combination of regions [Walker, 1969:893]—evidence that the communication and visibility patterns associated with location have a significant impact on the innovative behavior of the states. There are a number of instances when states load on factors composed of states that are predominantly outside their region, but Walker, while acknowledging this, reasonably contends that a pattern of regionalism still exists.

The fundamental question that should be asked at this point is whether these regional groupings are really the result of reference-group interaction and regularized search procedures or whether the similarity of within-group behavior is caused by common characteristics shared independently by the states. Do Arkansas and Alabama adopt various policies at about the same time because they communicate with each other continuously (a diffusion or interaction explanation) or because they are so similar (in terms of problems, resources, culture, etc.) that they would do pretty much the same thing even if there was no communication between them? Doubtless the similar behavior of two states such as these is a result of *both* their possessing many of the same socioeconomic and political characteristics and the fact that each pays attention to what the other is doing. It is also probably true that common characteristics and a high degree of interaction are mutually reinforcing, thereby making it still more difficult to disentangle the impact of each. Certainly, before we can really begin to answer this question we need to acquire more information about the communication and search patterns of state legislators and professionals.

Virginia Gray's [1973] follow-up article to Walker's is somewhat similar to the sort of treatment we might expect of an economist in the tradition of Mansfield and is only obliquely related to the question of what characteristics of states are responsible for their varying rates of innovativeness. The major portion of her essay is devoted to the analysis and comparison of policy diffusion curves primarily to test their congruence with the cumulative normal curve (an S-curve similar to the logistic) that characterizes the diffusion of so many innovations in a variety of areas. She finds the degree of similarity fairly high and concludes that a theory based on user interaction provides a satisfactory description of the diffusion process. This finding is important because it adds more weight to the argument that the kinds of communication and reference patterns stressed by Walker must be specified in order to understand variations in the states' adoption of policies. It also supplies us with more justification for applying innovation theory to policy analysis since policy innovations seem to diffuse like any other innovation.

Gray goes to some length to show that the innovativeness of states varies from one issue area to another but devotes little space to speculating why this is the case. Thus, although she demonstrates that first adopters are wealthier and more politically competitive than their sister states, she does not tell us why states are only intermittently first adopters or why the entire order of adoption varies, beyond intimating that the pattern of user interaction is unstable across issue areas.

Still, the variability in the order in which states adopt new policies does suggest that one or both of the following may be taking place:

1. *The score a state receives on a determinant changes from innovation to innovation;* for example, the state legislature might be interested in one innovation but not another, or the locus of decision for a given state in connection with one innovation may be the bureaucracy, but in another it could be the governor's office.
2. *Determinants have a different impact across innovations;* for example, per capita income might affect educational innovation but not criminal law innovation, or interest groups might have a greater impact on innovative policy in the area of welfare than in civil rights.

These reiterate two themes that appeared in Chapter 1: the need to focus on the choice setting and process (i.e., to be innovation specific in variable scoring) and the difficulties involved in fashioning a unitary theory of public policy formation or innovation.

Collier and Messick [1975], heavily influenced by Walker but much more familiar with determinants research than with organization theory, set out to test the superiority of a functional-prerequisites approach versus a diffusion explanation of social security adoption across nations. Basically, they seek to answer the question raised in connection with Walker's research of whether similar adoptive behavior is the result of common characteristics (a prerequisites explanation) or of communication and imitation (a diffusion explanation). Their findings prove to be provocative:

Among the earliest adopters, social security actually diffuses up a hierarchy of nations rather than down a hierarchy. In the middle group of adopters, a pattern of spatial diffusion is present in which social security is rapidly diffused among countries of widely differing levels of modernization. Finally, a combination of hierarchical diffusion and a prerequisites explanation appear to be the most satisfactory means of accounting for the pattern of adoption among the latest adopters [Collier and Messick, 1975:1314].

Curiously, Collier and Messick conclude their analysis at this point by expressing the hope that subsequent comparative research will consider the role of diffusion in political change. Readers are left to deal as best they can with a conclusion that implies that it may be necessary to adopt a different theory of innovation every twenty years or so. No speculations are made as to why the early group of adopters behaves in one way, the middle group in another way, and the late adopters in still a third way. If this is the best it can do, one might be fairly skeptical of any claims that a diffusion model will yield a significant payoff in terms of explanation or prediction.

While the relative importance of communication and imitation patterns as opposed to relatively intrinsic characteristics of the organization or policy (e.g., the level of resources) in determining adoptive behavior is a legitimate and interesting question, one wonders about both the necessity and wisdom of distinguishing so strongly between a prerequisites and a diffusion theory in trying to answer it. While a few variables associated with a prerequisites explanation (e.g., GNP, literacy) may be largely independent of the effects of those variables that characterize the diffusion process, many are not. For instance, it is not difficult to imagine the proximity of one state to another and the level of communication between them affecting the values and perceptions of both mass public and elites—variables that should legitimately be included in a prerequisites model. Perhaps the appropriate course is to integrate characteristics of the diffusion process directly into what Collier and Messick consider to be a prerequisites model. This could be done by creating variables which specify the distance between units, frequency of contact, degree of centrality in the social network and so forth. The possibility of integrating elements of the diffusion model into a prerequisites model indicates that they are really not alternative explanatory models at all but, rather, represent complementary ways of presenting the same data which emphasize different categories of variables.

Collier and Messick unwittingly add credence to the desirability of abandoning the absolute distinction between the approaches at one point by attempting to explain the upward diffusion of social security among early adopters on the basis of what amounts to a difference in the ideologies of two groups of nations. They attribute it to the weaker development of the liberal tradition of self-reliance in Germany, Austria, and Hungary as compared to England, Denmark, the Netherlands, and France [Collier and Messick, 1975:1311]. If ideology were incorporated in a prerequisites model, it would presumably fit the data as well as any diffusion model. Furthermore, if diffusion model variables were included, we would observe a high degree of multicollinearity between ideology and communication pattern or location, which would lead us to speculate on the nature of the causal relationship between them.

In addition, should we postulate the existence of interaction among the explanatory variables in the prerequisites model (like Mohr), we realize that the enormous amount of variation that generally move Collier and Messick to dismiss the necessary-prerequisites model in favor of a diffusion model would, in fact, not be inconsistent with it and would provide little justification for its abandonment. Their test of a necessary-prerequisites model, which consists of looking at the variation a variable exhibits across cases, is only valid if we assume the relationship among variables is additive. If we assume that there is a multiplicative relationship between motivation and resources, it would be possible that the very low per capita income of one adopter might have been compensated for by some other variable—perhaps an ideological variable that measures motivation. If this is the case, we cannot say that per capita income doesn't matter—potentially it could matter quite a bit—only that its impact is conditional.

In summary, none of the studies have had a great deal to say about the specific characteristics of states or nations that are responsible for policy innovation. In each case the number of explanatory variables included in the analysis is quite small, and those that were selected are identical to those commonly found in the determinants studies described in Chapter 1. They do not include elite or bureaucratic characteristics; nor do they explore the issue of interaction. Nevertheless, the application of innovation theory to the field of public policy has produced some interesting results.

First, research has shown that policy innovations behave like other innovations, at least with respect to their diffusion curves. We really do not know whether the similarity extends to the determinants of their adoption, although we suspect that it will if we can identify comparable dimensions across the diverse units of analysis. Second, because policy innovations diffuse like other innovations, we have good reason to believe that patterns of communication and imitation are important determinants of adoption. All of the articles cited stress this, although in each case the author was unable to comment conclusively about the importance of communication as compared with other variables. For that matter, the essential attributes of the communication and imitation process remained unidentified. Still, these studies represent the first empirical research on policy determinants to recognize the potential significance of characteristics of the diffusion process in explaining the variation in policy adoption.

Finally, because the application of innovation theory provides determinants researchers with a more or less specific set of expectations, important spillover benefits occur when the analysts (and the reader) are forced to account for deviations in these expectations. For example, Walker's [1969] view of regional identification and its implications becomes increasingly deeper and more interesting as he considers those states, like New York and California, that load on more than one factor. Similarly, the erosion he discovers in regional groupings over time leads him to speculate on the growing importance of professional groups in fostering innovation [Walker, 1969:894–95]. This further sensitizes us to the need for operationalizing concepts and measuring variables that have never been included in conventional determinants research.

The Innovation: Deinstitutionalization in Juvenile Corrections

Shortly after I took office, I became convinced that there were better ways to deal with juvenile offenders. Programs which would certainly prove more effective than shutting them away in institutions. I felt that a community-based treatment system would provide better rehabilitative services and still cost less to the taxpayers of Massachusetts.

—Francis W. Sargent,
Governor of Massachusetts, 1971

As stated in the Introduction, deinstitutionalization represents the shift from incarcerating adjudicated juveniles in large, relatively "closed" and predominantly custodial institutions—often officially designated as training schools and popularly known as reform schools—to placing them in smaller, more open, community-based facilities called group homes and halfway houses. A similar movement is presently taking place in the area of mental health. The widespread development and utilization of community-based programs as an alternative to institutionalization is a very recent phenomenon, although, as in the case of many policy innovations, the basic idea has been around for a very long time. In 1971 there were only 705 juvenile offenders placed in group homes and halfway houses [U.S. NCJISS, 1974] as compared to 5,300 on an average day in 1974. The difference between the two figures is actually even more dramatic than it appears, since the 1971 total almost certainly includes a large percentage of juveniles who had been previously institutionalized and were paroled to the community-based facility as a stage in the reintegration process (hence the derivation of the term *halfway* house). This percentage was almost certainly smaller in 1974, by which time it had become more common practice to assign a youth to a community facility *in lieu* of institutional placement.

The policy of deinstitutionalization has been justified on a number of grounds, but almost invariably these center around the criticism of traditional juvenile institutions. There appears to be wide consensus that in general these facilities have been ineffective, too expensive, inhumane, and operated under a custodial philosophy that places institutional maintenance goals far above rehabilitative ones.

The failure of major institutions to reduce crime is incontestable. Recidivism rates are notoriously high. Institutions do succeed in punishing, but they do not deter.

They protect the community, but that protection is only temporary. They relieve the community of responsibility by removing the offender, but they make success-ful reintegration into the community unlikely. They change the committed of-fender, but the change is more likely to be negative than positive. . . . Our institutions are so large that their operational needs take precedence over the needs of the people they hold. The very scale of these institutions dehumanizes, denies privacy, encourages violence, and defies decent control [National Advi-sory Commission, 1973:1 and 12].

Although the evidence concerning the relative effectiveness of community-based programs as compared to institutions in terms of re-cidivism is extremely equivocal, it is commonly argued that they reduce the probability of recidivism by providing the offender with a stable and supportive environment within the same community to which the juvenile must eventually adapt. In addition to this assertion that community facil-ities foster normalization, proponents also argue that these programs are more humane, less stigmatizing, less likely to function as schools of crime, and, of particular importance, less expensive.

The entire case is summarized nicely in the following excerpt from Florida's *Comprehensive Plan, 1974–1980* [Florida Division of Youth Services, 1974:15]:

Community-based corrections is one of the most promising developments in corrections today. It is based on the recognition that a considerable amount of delinquency and crime is a symptom of failure of the community, as well as the offender, and that a successful reduction of crime requires changes in both. Reasons for embracing the concept of community corrections and for embarking on a national strategy to effect a transition from our current institution-oriented correctional system to one that is community-based include the following:
—There is convincing evidence that current use of and practices in the traditional penal institutions intensify and compound the problems they profess to correct.
—The cost of institutionalization, particularly with the system's current excessive emphasis on security and hardware, is reaching a magnitude beyond all reason.
—The majority of offenders currently are treated as violent and dangerous despite the fact that only a few of them conform to this unfortunate stereotype.
—Time spent in confinement is inversely related to success on parole, and community-based programs appear to be more effective than traditional institu-tional programs in providing community protection.
—Imprisonment has a negative effect on an offender's ability to develop sufficient skills and competence to perform culturally prescribed roles after release into the community.
—The move toward community corrections implies that communities must as-sume responsibility for the problems that in part originate at the community level.

The policy of deinstitutionalization is not without its opponents, although one is hard-pressed to find any criticism in articles or books by academics or professionals in the field. The criticism that does exist is not so much directed against the principle of community corrections as it is against those who faddishly assert that such programs are the "final solution" for the rehabilitation of all offenders. Those academics and professionals who are skeptical about the efficacy of the movement to community corrections contend that it specifies no new and coherent technology of rehabilitation.

> Following on the heels of the rejection of the institution as a setting for meaningful behavior change is a too ready acceptance of the notion that all one needs to do is to move corrections out of the institution and into the community and all will be well. Under current conditions, what this consists of is old wine in new bottles [Quay, 1975:5].

Some of the most common bases for opposition to deinstitutionalization are not directly related to the relative effectiveness of community-based facilities, nor do they fill the pages of academic or professional journals. Rather, they mirror the diverse concerns and values of interested individuals and groups and reinforce the difficulty of providing a unitary definition of "worth" for an issue area in the public sector.

As might be expected, there are those who oppose deinstitutionalization on the grounds that the commitment of offenders to community programs in which they retain a moderate degree of personal freedom amounts to "coddling" them, when they should be punished. There are also those who want the courts to remove troublemakers from the community. They can include neighbors, school officials, police, and, not infrequently, the parents of offenders themselves. The highest priority of these individuals and groups is neither rehabilitation nor punishment but the absolute assurance that there will be no recurrence of the behavior for a significant period of time. The advocates of "removal" view community programming with a jaundiced eye and justify their position by appealing to the need for community protection.[h] Finally (although this list is by no means exhaustive), some of the most persistent opposition to deinstitutionalization comes from teachers, social workers, and maintenance and custodial personnel who have been working in juvenile institutions for many years and have a vested interest in their continuing operation. These groups stand to lose power, status, and perhaps even their jobs. They are increasingly undergoing unionization, which provides them with the resources and cohesion to engage in concerted efforts to prevent the redistribution of correctional funds from institutions to community-based programs.

---

[h]The issue of increased community vulnerability under a system of community-based incarceration is a salient and complex one. It is noteworthy, however, that a large proportion of juveniles are adjudicated delinquent for crimes that are *not* against persons or even property (e.g., truancy, running away, prostitution).

37

Operationalizing Innovativeness: The Dependent Variable

In this study a state's deinstitutionalization rate was calculated by dividing the number of offenders placed in state-operated, or state-funded, community-based residential facilities by the total number of offenders in these facilities plus those in institutions. This yields the proportion of incarcerated offenders who are in community facilities and, when multiplied by 100, gives that proportion as a percentage. The scores for the forty-eight states capable of providing this data are presented in Table 2–4. Figure 2–1 portrays the same information somewhat more dramatically.

Table 2–4
Deinstitutionalization: Percent Offenders in Community-Based Residential Programs of the Number of Offenders in Community-Based Programs, Institutions, Camps, and Ranches

Massachusetts	86.6	Pennsylvania	11.7
South Dakota	59.1	Colorado	11.4
Minnesota	50.9	Kentucky	10.8
Utah	50.3	Mississippi	9.0
Oregon	48.6	West Virginia	8.8
North Dakota	43.4	Tennessee	8.6
Maryland	42.0	Oklahoma	8.3
Kansas	41.5	Illinois	8.2
Idaho	30.4	Rhode Island	7.4
Michigan	28.5	Ohio	6.3
Florida	25.2	Georgia	3.7
Montana	25.0	Delaware	3.6
Wyoming	24.7	South Carolina	3.5
Vermont	23.8	Arkansas	3.2
Arizona	20.8	California	2.9
Connecticut	20.6	Texas	2.8
New Jersey	17.7	Maine	2.0
Alabama	17.0	Nebraska	1.5
Missouri	14.8	Alaska	0
Hawaii	13.6	Indiana	0
Nevada	13.0	Louisiana	0
Iowa	12.9	New Hampshire	0
Wisconsin	12.4	New Mexico	0
Virginia	12.0	North Carolina	0

An alternative to using deinstitutionalization rate as the dependent variable would have been to employ the "number of offenders in community-based facilities per capita" as a measure of the degree to which a state is innovative in this area. However, deinstitutionalization rate as operationalized above was thought to be the superior, for several reasons. First, community corrections is viewed in the literature as an alternative rather than as merely a supplement to institutional commit-

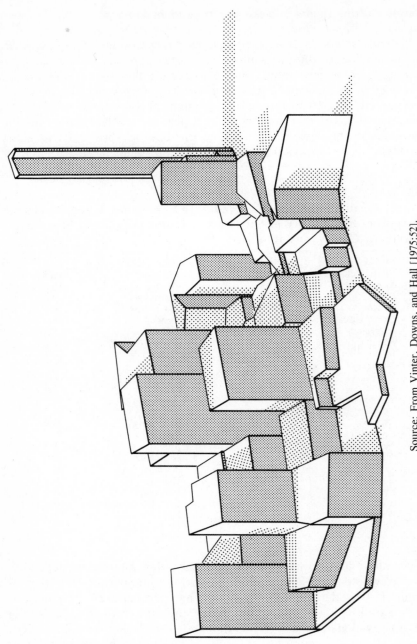

Source: From Vinter, Downs, and Hall [1975:52].

Figure 2–1. Deinstitutionalization Rates.

ment. Deinstitutionalization rate is more sensitive to this reordering of programming priorities that is at the heart of the innovation since it is a measure of *distribution*: A state will receive a higher score if it *reduces* its institutional population *in addition to* increasing the number of offenders in community programs.

Furthermore, because deinstitutionalization rate is an indicator of the degree of priority redistribution that has taken place, there is some reason to expect that its determinants are similar to those of other policy innovations that also involve the redistribution of scarce resources (e.g., open housing and affirmative action). In the case of each of these relatively zero-sum rather than purely expanding-sum innovations, it is necessary to know not only the absolute number of houses occupied by blacks or the number of jobs held by women or minorities, but also the figures as proportions of the base number of houses or jobs available.

Deinstitutionalization rate is a measure of the *extent* to which a state is committed to community-based programs and, as such, it is a rather unusual operationalization of adoption. By far the most common procedure for determining the innovativeness of states or organizations is to assign a score that reflects the date when the innovation was first used or, as in Walker's [1969] study, the date when the enabling legislation was passed. Although this method of scoring produces an interesting ordering of adopting units, it does not differentiate between "superficial" and "deep" adoption—that is, it reveals nothing about the extent to which the innovation has been employed, and frequently it is the determinants of this extent that are really of interest. Returning to the policy innovation of affirmative action, while it is useful to know what determined the order in which states or cities adopted the policy, it is much more desirable that the researcher uncover what determines the extent to which the principles of the policy are applied.

The question of what determines the degree to which an innovation is actually implemented is rarely dealt with in the literature,[i] although it has occasionally been the practice to set a threshold of commitment that must be attained before a unit is said to have adopted the innovation.

The fact that the vast majority of studies of innovation have concerned themselves exclusively with the date of the initial adoption— usually setting no threshold other than "first usage"—is theoretically significant only if it was suspected that the determinants of the time of adoption differed from those of the extent of adoption, either in terms of the makeup of the determinants, the interaction between them, or their individual effects. However, this suspicion seems quite reasonable. For example, because a certain amount of prestige accrues to the individuals

---

[i]Griliches [1957] is the notable exception.

or organizations that are among the first to adopt a new innovation, we might hypothesize that the desire for prestige will be a more powerful predictor of the time of adoption than of the extent of adoption. Organizational wealth (slack) might also be a better predictor of how quickly an organization adopts an innovation than of how extensively the innovation is employed—something that may depend heavily on motivational variables.

If it is true that the determinants of the date of adoption differ from those of the extent of adoption, we would expect that innovation scores of the units involved would vary depending on the measure used. Although no one has systematically collected the data, there is every reason to believe that if the states were ordered by the date on which they first established a group home, the list would look quite different than Table 2–4. States like California, New York, and Illinois would be ranked much higher, while Arizona, South Dakota, and Florida would be ranked somewhat lower. This may help to explain the somewhat modest correlation (.26) between state deinstitutionalization rates and Walker's index of general state innovativeness. It is hoped that the results reported in the following chapters will indicate some of the ways in which the almost exclusive reliance on time of adoption may bias our perception of the organizational attributes that lead to innovativeness.

A serious methodological problem is at issue here also. If units are scored solely on the basis of time of adoption, the potential problem arises of their having adopted what amount to different innovations. Is a farmer who experimentally plants 10 acres of hybrid corn on his 1,000-acre farm engaging in the same innovative behavior as one who initially plants 900 acres of hybrid corn? And are we willing to believe that the variables that determine the initial adoption of a usage rate of 1 percent are the same that determine a usage rate of 90 percent?

As stated in the Introduction, the problem of a common label concealing important and systematic diversities should not be present here. Obviously, community-based programs are not all exactly the same: Some are more restrictive than others, they employ different therapies, they can contain different types of offenders, and they can have differing levels of resources at their disposal. But the variation of community-based programs appears to be as great within states as between them, and their similarity in terms of size, location, restrictions on offenders, and guiding philosophies is strong.

Overall, deinstitutionalization rate appears to possess a number of attributes that make it an attractive and interesting dependent variable for an exploratory study of the impact of bureaucracy on the adoption of policy innovation:

1. It reflects a major programmatic innovation that is recognized as such by corrections personnel and interest groups in all fifty states.
2. As operationalized, it measures the degree to which the innovation has been implemented and thus distinguishes between token or superficial adoption and "authentic" adoption.
3. It is a ratio-level variable, subject to little measurement error.
4. The innovation it represents has diffused quickly and has already been extensively implemented in a number of states (e.g., Massachusetts is 86 percent deinstitutionalized).
5. Unlike many policy measures, it is not based on expenditures and therefore not subject to the drawbacks of such measures [LeMay, 1973].

A Summary of Related Research Issues

In addition to initiating an empirical exploration into the impact of the bureaucracy and its immediate environment on public policy, the chapters that follow tentatively address a number of the issues that have been raised in the preceding pages. All of these issues are clearly relevant to the main thrust of this study, but they are also of considerable interest in themselves to students of innovation. For this reason they have been singled out below. The adverb *tentatively* is not included for reasons of self-effacement; in looking down the list it is apparent that it would be impossible to even provisionally settle these issues on the basis of a single study. They are included because there are data that are relevant to them and because they are worth thinking about.

First, will the structural variables so central to the sociological tradition have any significant impact on adoption when motivational and environmental variables are included in the analysis? What is their relative importance, and how do they interact with other variables? The findings described in the determinants literature and the increasing prevalence of "consonance" or "contingency" hypotheses[j] in the literature of organization theory suggest that they may be closely related to environmental characteristics and their impact conditional on them. Moreover, are variables such as complexity and hierarchy the dimensions of organizational structure that deserve our attention, or should we be looking at those dimensions of decision making that have largely been ignored, like decision and information costs, and decision autonomy?

---

[j]That is, that the impact of structural variables varies depending on characteristics of the environment [Mohr, 1971].

Second, in the murky area of what motivates public sector organizations to adopt policy innovations, what is the role of executive ideology, professional values, and environmental pressures? Do motivations interact with resources in the way Mohr [1969] contends? Do motivational variables assume greater importance when the innovation in question (as is the case here) involves a budget redistribution as well as perhaps an increase?

Third, and this is closely related to the second issue, what elements go into a public bureaucracy's definition of "worth" in an area where objective evaluative criteria are absent or do not discriminate between policy alternatives? What part of this definition can be traced directly to the ideologies of the bureaucracy's decisionmakers, and what part is traceable back to the values and priorities of prominent actors in the environment (recognizing that there is interaction between the two groups)? Where evaluative criteria are absent, personal and professional values may have to be the centerpiece of research—but whose? Does expected profit have a simple analog in the public sector?

Fourth, what happens to the impact of those variables commonly included in adoption models when innovation is measured by the extent of implementation or commitment as opposed to the time of adoption? Does there seem to be any empirical justification for the development of two separate models?

Fifth, what dimensions of the public sector organization's environment are the principle determinants of adoption? Do characteristics of the general ecological environment of state bureaucracies (e.g., per capita income, urbanization, crime rates) appear to possess more or less explanatory power than characteristics of the more immediate organizational and political environment that are potentially generalizable from one issue area to another—size? complexity? instability?

Sixth, and last, how can knowledge of the communication and imitation patterns that exist in a policy area help explain variation in innovation rates among units? What are the generalizable dimensions of the communication and imitation processes that can be integrated into a "prerequisite model" of innovation, and what is their relative impact? What role do professional groups play in these processes?

3

The Impact of Socioeconomic Characteristics

On the basis of most of the studies described in the first chapter, one would anticipate that socioeconomic characteristics would explain a major portion of the variance in state deinstitutionalization rates. In fact, that literature suggests that in terms of explained variance this will be the most revealing chapter, with subsequent ones on the task environments of correctional bureaucracies and their internal characteristics yielding only incremental gains—if any. One need only recall the "disappointing" results of Falcone and Whittington's [1972] ambitious and thoughtful attempt to overturn the new orthodoxy by carefully specifying and measuring the political components of the black box. While it is true that recent research [Fry and Winters, 1970; LeMay, 1973; Booms and Halldorson, 1973] might lead us to anticipate that the relative impact of socioeconomic variables may vary across policy areas, there is no empirical justification for anticipating that the explanatory power of these variables will be anything less than substantial; nor has any rigorous theoretical argument been put forth in the literature which would lead us to question this expectation.

Research by Walker [1971] and Gray [1973] on the determinants and diffusion of policy innovations further substantiates this view. Walker's discovery of a series of zero-order correlations approaching .60 between his innovation index and percent urban, total population, per capita income, value added per capita by manufacturing, and average value per acre of farms led him to conclude that socioeconomic development was a key determinant of state innovativeness [Walker, 1969:884]. Gray, after examining a number of individual innovations and the characteristics of the states that first adopted them similarly observed that her findings were consistent with the hypotheses derived from studies of state and local expenditures [Gray, 1973:1182].

Yet it is important to review the theoretical case for anticipating a close connection between a policy innovation like deinstitutionalization and economic development. From a theoretical standpoint, how justified are we in predicting that the results of most determinants research will hold in this instance? The answer to this question, as will become apparent, is a tentative "not very." But, before we can reasonably make a meaningful prediction about the impact of socioeconomic characteristics on deinstitutionalization on theoretical grounds, it is necessary to carefully explore what is meant by "socioeconomic environment" and how it is thought to "shape" policy outputs.

43

Although dealing with these issues should be a normal prelude to hypothesis formation, they can easily be overlooked or brushed aside. The high degree of face validity and deceptive simplicity of the assertion that socioeconomic characteristics affect policy has a tendency to pre-empt discussion about—and further research into—the precise nature of that impact. This is ironic since to a large extent determinants research began as an iconoclastic critique of certain unexamined assumptions regarding the impact of political structures and processes on policy. It would be unfortunate if that small body of theory that is gradually being built up became similarly marred by hasty generalizations about the role of a potpourri of variables broadly termed the environment.

Dimensionality and Socioeconomic Variables

Possibly because of the initial notoriety the field of comparative policy analysis gained by examining the relative impacts of socioeconomic and political characteristics, the former have always been lumped together for purposes of analysis and discussion. Even now dialogue in the field continues to be structured by the original issue of the relative explanatory power of the "socioeconomic environment" as a whole [Fried, 1973; Booms and Halldorson, 1973]. Although individual coefficients are presented for each socioeconomic variable included in the analysis, it is their joint impact (e.g., their multiple R^2) that receives the bulk of the attention. While it has become common practice to compare the total amount of variance that can be explained by socioeconomic attributes in one policy area with the amount they explain in another policy area, researchers rarely comment at length about the differing impacts of particular variables. If socioeconomic variables account for 30 percent of the variance in connection with each of two policy outputs, the impact of the socioeconomic environment is considered to be equivalent regardless of the respective composition of the socioeconomic "factors" and what can amount to variations in the loadings of the individual variables that make them up. The fact that per capita income accounts for two-thirds of the explained variance in one case but less than a third in the other tends to go unnoticed as long as the variations in the predictive power of other socioeconomic variables function to produce similar composite R^2s. The field's primary interest, understandably enough considering its origins, has always been in the total extent to which policy is determined by characteristics that are exogenous to the political system and basically nonmanipulatable (at least in the short term) by policymakers.

If we could be confident that the environment could be adequately characterized by a single dimension such as economic development, there would be no compelling reason to modify the practice of devoting all attention toward the composite impact of socioeconomic characteristics. However, not only do there appear to be important dimensions of the socioeconomic environment that are not captured by the concept of economic development, but that term itself appears to be ambiguous aggregation of several distinct dimensions.

At some time in the past a nation's, state's, or city's economic development might have been validly and equivalently characterized by either the level of per capita income, urbanization, or industrialization.[a] Yet, as Hofferbert and his colleagues have shown [Cameron et al., 1972, 1975], the interrelationship among these variables has deteriorated (if it once existed) to the point where a factor analysis of both comparative *and* longitudinal data places industrialization on a dimension that is orthogonal to that on which per capita income and urbanization are found. No statistical sleight of hand is at work here; the variables load very heavily on the positive end of their respective factors and maintain their loadings in developing as well as postindustrial nations. Examples of differences in the American states between the level of industrialization and per capita income are plentiful.

North Carolina, which was thirty-fourth in industrialization in 1890, was eighteenth in 1960; nevertheless, it moved downward from forty-second to forty-sixth in affluence in the same period. Conversely, though Montana dropped from twenty-sixth to forty-fourth in industrialization, it remained one of the most affluent states. Compared to New Jersey, Michigan, and Illinois, the states of the Plains and Rocky Mountains are not industrialized. Yet Nevada has one of the highest levels of income and education in the country. Wyoming, too, can not be considered as economically "underdeveloped," despite its lack of factories [Hofferbert, 1972:13].

Once the unidimensional concept of economic development is revealed to be an oversimplification that is statistically unjustified, it is appropriate to speculate about the theoretical richness that has been lost by treating socioeconomic attributes en masse. To date, few hypotheses have been generated about the particular policy consequences of such potentially key attributes of social structure as racial and ethnic heterogeneity, income distribution, religious affiliation, industrial differentiation, or mobility patterns, despite their regular inclusion in the list of variables used to calculate the total impact of the socioeconomic environment.[b] There is still a larger number of variables, ranging from cultural norms to

---

[a]This may still be true in certain underdeveloped areas—such as non–Moslem Africa—that do not have a long tradition of nonindustrial urbanization.

[b]Partial exceptions to the above are Aiken and Alford [1970], Hofferbert [1968, 1972], Sharkansky and Hofferbert [1969], and Cameron et al. [1975].

the conditions under which states first intervened in a particular policy area, whose importance has been stressed by members of other social science disciplines [e.g., Stinchcombe, 1965], but upon which data have not been collected.

Since attributes of the environment have commonly been lumped together for purposes of comparison with political characteristics and because they were assumed to represent the single dimension of economic development, very little theory has been developed about the manner in which any single variable shapes different categories of policy. For example, despite the fact that industrialization has been included in countless studies, relatively few specific conclusions have been generated about its impact on policy. Does it affect welfare policy more than educational policy? Can its impact be expected to be greater on the rate and scope of policy innovation than on total expenditures? The fact that there is no emergent body of theory from which to generate tentative answers to such questions hinders the researcher's ability to meaningfully estimate the magnitude of the relationship that will be uncovered between industrialization and a given policy output.

Predictions Based on Past Research

Since aside from an implicit acceptance of the fact that economic development is related to policy development virtually no theory has been generated about the impact of particular socioeconomic characteristics on policy, there is little basis for forming hypotheses about the relationship of specific variables to deinstitutionalization other than previous research. Because there is a general consensus that the effect of socioeconomic variables varies somewhat across policy areas,[c] only the results of the studies most closely related to this one are given in Table 3–1. Walker's [1969] study of state innovativeness, a logical selection, has already been described. The other set of findings comes from Booms and Halldorson's [1973:930] correction and extension of Fry and Winters's article on the determinants of redistribution. Like deinstitutionalization, their dependent variable—a redistribution index—is a distributional measure rather than a straight measure of expenditures and is made up of outputs directed essentially at have-not populations.

The findings in Table 3–1 are generally consistent with both the expectations of those who conducted the research and with the determi-

[c]While there is empirical evidence that this is true, only two explanations have been offered: (1) the more distantly related the output is to expenditures, the less socioeconomic variables matter; and (2) socioeconomic variables are less important when political variables become more important. Neither is especially satisfying.

Table 3–1

Relationship of Socioeconomic Variables to Walker's Innovation Index and Booms and Halldorson's Redistribution Index

	Walker's Innovation Index	Booms and Halldorson's Redistribution Index
Income	.55	.65
Industrialization	.66	.43
Urbanization	.63	.67
Education	.29	.39
	R^2 not reported	$R^2 = .56$

nants literature surveyed in Chapter 1. They strongly imply that the combined explanatory power of these four traditional measures of socioeconomic development with respect to state deinstitutionalization rates will be considerable. More importantly, an examination of the individual correlations can be used as a basis upon which to formulate relatively precise hypotheses about the magnitude of the impact that each will have on the dependent variable. For example, rather than say only that we anticipate there will be a positive correlation between income and deinstitutionalization, we can now estimate that the strength of the relationship will be somewhere in the range of .55 to .65. It should be noted that these individual correlations suggest that the effect of urbanization is likely to be much greater than education, which conflicts with the assumption that each of the variables is an equivalent indicator of development.

Alternative Expectations

There are a number of reasons for anticipating that the variables listed in Table 3–1 will not relate to the policy of deinstitutionalization at the same magnitude as Walker's innovativeness index or Booms and Halldorson's reformulated index of redistribution. Because these variables are not all closely interrelated,[d] it is desirable to reflect on the potential impact of each individually rather than to speculate about the effect of the

---

[d]The four variables are intercorrelated in the following way:

	Per Capita Income	Industrialization	Median Education	Percent Urban
Per capita income	1.00			
Industrialization	.23	1.00		
Median education	.66	−.29	1.00	
Percent urban	.61	.54	.26	1.00

socioeconomic environment as a whole. However, before this can be done, a brief digression is necessary.

Delinquency Rate

Each of the four variables is moderately related to the level of delinquency that exists in the states.[e] This raises the possibility that each may have a crucial indirect effect on deinstitutionalization through its relationship to delinquency rate. It will therefore simplify the following discussion if we can deal once and for all with the link between the amount of delinquency within a state and the level of deinstitutionalization.

Initially, one might expect delinquency to be strongly related to deinstitutionalization, on the grounds that a high crime rate on the part of juveniles (especially recidivists) will generate pressure on the state agency responsible for juvenile corrections to propose an innovative way to rehabilitate offenders or, minimally, to "do something." However, a countervailing argument contends that increased juvenile crime creates a climate of public opinion in which the values of punitive retribution and community protection are salient and that these are hostile to the development of rehabilitatively oriented, community-based programs.

In addition, the fact that the rehabilitative value of community-based programs is largely unknown reduces the probability that states will automatically move toward deinstitutionalization as juvenile crime increases. Few of the quotations included in Chapter 2 that advocated the initiation of community-based programs contained any reference to crime rate, nor did interviews of agency executives reveal any indication of a relationship between the amount or rate of increase in juvenile crime and their attitude toward deinstitutionalization. Thus, there appears to be no compelling reason to expect either a positive or a negative relationship between delinquency and deinstitutionalization. Having said this, we can now proceed to consider other arguments that link the four socioeconomic variables to the dependent variable.

Income

The classic rationale for anticipating a positive relationship between organizational wealth or "slack" and innovativeness has been formulated by Cyert and March [1963:278]:

---

[e]The precise size of the correlations varies considerably, depending on whether one measures delinquency by the number of youths adjudicated or by the number of property crimes (the most common youthful offense) reported.

One of the main consequences of slack is a muting of problems of scarcity. Subunit demands are less closely reviewed (since they are less likely to conflict with other demands). Resources are more likely to be allocated if they are sought strongly by a single subunit. Thus, distributed slack is available for projects that would not necessarily be approved in a tight budget.

Walker and others have drawn upon this basic argument to provide theoretical support for the hypothesis that indicators of organizational slack are major determinants of public sector innovativeness.

If "slack" resources are available, either in the form of money or a highly skilled, professional staff, the decision maker can afford the luxury of experiment and can more easily risk the possibility of failure [Walker, 1969:883].

However, there are several reasons why the relationship between per capita income and deinstitutionalization is likely to be weaker than that between income and Walker's innovation index. First, the fact that deinstitutionalization is at least partly a redistributive innovation that will, according to its proponents, reduce correctional expenditures would seem to attenuate the impact of state wealth. While significant start-up costs appear to be associated with the development of community-based programs, a substantial proportion of the funds necessary to cover these costs can be procured from the federal government through the Law Enforcement Assistance Administration (LEAA).

Second, implicit in the hypothesis that high per capita income will lead to bureaucratic innovativeness is the assumption that wealthy states possess wealthy state agencies. Yet this assumption turns out to be quite tenuous. The zero-order correlation between *all* state expenditures (per capita) and per capita income is a modest .39, which by itself throws some doubt on the prevalent assumption that per capita income is a good indicator of governmental slack. The correlation between juvenile corrections agency expenditures for all types of residential programs (which account for the bulk of agencies' expenditures and is the only comparable basis for comparison) and income is even less, at .25. Thus the juvenile corrections agencies in wealthy states are simply not that more likely to have a larger budget to spend on innovations or on the hiring of innovation-oriented professionals.

Third, for the reasons suggested in Chapter 2, it is probable that wealth and slack are more important factors in determining the *time* at which a state adopts and the *number* of innovations it adopts than in determining the *extent* to which it adopts a given innovation. Because Walker's index is sensitive to the speed and frequency of innovative behavior, while deinstitutionalization is a measure of the *depth* of that behavior, we would expect per capita income to be more closely related to the former.

Urbanization

Aside from any impact through its effect on per capita income or median education, one might suspect urbanization to be strongly related to deinstitutionalization because community correctional programs were basically designed as treatment alternatives for urban youth. However, because delinquency is also primarily an urban phenomenon, such programs are neither more nor less applicable to the delinquent populations of rural states, which can be expected to come from the urban portions of those states. There is no reason to believe that less urbanized states will necessarily have a lower *ratio* of youth in community facilities to youth in institutions, only that they will have *fewer* community-based programs.

Industrialization

There would seem to be no theoretical reason for hypothesizing any relationship between industrialization and deinstitutionalization except as industrialization is related to some other socioeconomic characteristic thought to be relevant, such as education (see following section). Industrialization provides another good example of the likely differential effect of environmental variables on policy outputs. Although it can be logically related to pollution standards, minimum wage and fair trade law, and child labor standards, any direct and theoretically interesting relationship between industrialization and deinstitutionalization, teacher certification requirements, or open-housing legislation is obscure at best.

Education

There are at least two ways in which the level of education in a state might affect the extent of deinstitutionalization. First, a better-educated citizenry would seem less likely to be content with the demonstrably ineffective, and often inhumane, incarceration of juveniles in institutions. We might expect higher levels of education to lead to greater political and social consciousness that would manifest itself in the sort of interest-group participation (e.g., League of Women Voters, ACLU) often associated with reform. Because causes involving youth are often the targets of these groups, the rehabilitation of delinquents would appear to be a logical focus for this activity. This line of reasoning leads to the hypothesis that a high level of education is associated with a greater amount of *demand* for innovative juvenile services.

Second, one expects that the better educated the population, the more tolerant it would be toward less punitive forms of treatment and the more receptive it would be toward the concept of treating deviancy *within* the community. The local population's acceptance of facilities like group homes and halfway houses is essential to the success of these programs. Not only is the reintegration of the offenders into the community the key to their treatment philosophy, but frequently the establishment of these facilities is contingent on the prior approval of people in the neighborhood. Following this reasoning, the absence of an educated population can be viewed as a *resource constraint* on policymakers who might otherwise be interested in innovating.

These two arguments suggest that deinstitutionalization will be related to median education. However, the strength of the relationship is unlikely to be more than moderate for several reasons. One is that the demand argument, although reasonable, is simply not that powerful. Juvenile corrections is only a peripheral concern for most interest groups. Another reason is that the nature of the functional form by which a resource constraint relates to a policy output can be expected to produce only a low to moderate correlation. To understand why this is the case, another digression is necessary.

The Functional Form of Relationships: A Digression

Figure 3–1 consists of a scatter diagram depicting the relationship between a policy output (P) and a socioeconomic variable (SE). The relationship shown is of the type that would be generated if SE were a

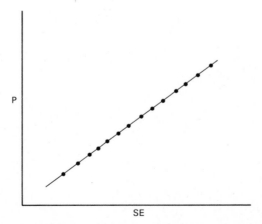

Figure 3–1. Scatter Plot Generated by Necessary and Sufficient Condition.

necessary and sufficient condition of P. SE relates to P as a necessary condition since the maximum level of P that a state can attain is a perfect linear function of its score on SE. In addition, because the minimum score any state receives on P consistently increases as SE increases, SE can be said to act as a sufficient condition of P. Thus, SE relates to P in the manner of a necessary and sufficient condition because at any point it appears to set both the upper and lower boundaries of the distribution of states on P.[f] The use of such logical and explicitly causal categories to describe the functional form of the "association" between two variables may appear pretentious, but the distinctions they represent turn out to be extremely useful in much of the analysis that is to follow.

If SE were a *sufficient* condition of P but not a necessary one, the functional form of the relationship would resemble that shown in Figure 3–2. That SE is a sufficient condition of P is again evidenced by the fact that as SE increases, the minimum score that any state receives on P also increases, However, because SE is no longer a necessary condition of P, many states achieve relatively high scores on P despite their low SE scores. This tells us that P is brought about by a factor or factors in

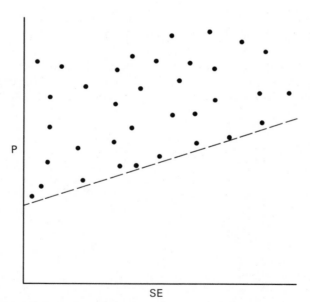

Figure 3–2. Scatter Plot Generated by Sufficient but Not Necessary Condition.

---

[f]In this case, of course, the upper and lower boundaries of the distribution are the same.

addition to SE. In this case SE determines the lower boundary of the distribution at a given point but not the upper boundary.

While few of the relationships uncovered by determinants researchers resemble Figure 3–1, many have a form similar to Figure 3–2.[g] Of course, this is to be expected since it is generally assumed that most policy outputs are a function of not one but several determinants and that each determinant is independently capable of bringing about an increase in the output to which it is related. For example, it is undoubtedly the case that a number of factors aside from an increase in unemployment can lead to increases in state welfare expenditures. Although we might well predict that the unemployment rate establishes a baseline for welfare expenditures and that this baseline rises in proportion to that rate (i.e., the unemployment rate determines the lower boundary of the distribution of states on welfare expenditures), we would still expect to find a number of states with large welfare budgets despite low unemployment.

It would, however, be incorrect to jump to the conclusion that when an output is the function of more than one determinant, every determinant relates to it as a sufficient but not necessary condition. It is possible that one or more determinants may be *necessary but not sufficient* conditions of the output, in which case the relationship would resemble the one in Figure 3–3. Here SE determines the upper boundary of the distribution of

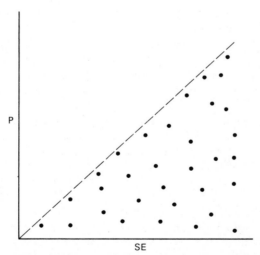

Figure 3–3. Scatter Plot Generated by Necessary but Not Sufficient Condition.

---

[g]For numerous examples see Dye [1966].

states on P but is unrelated to the lower boundary. SE restricts the maximum level of P that states can attain; however, a high score on SE is not sufficient to ensure that a state will achieve a high level of P.

Figure 3–3 seems to characterize the relationship that people have in mind when they speak of some environmental attribute functioning as a *resource constraint* with respect to a particular output. For example, it provides a pictorial summary of the position of those comparativists who believe that socioeconomic development provides resources necessary for the attainment of viable democratic institutions but does not guarantee that they will emerge [Neubauer 1967]. We might also anticipate that such a plot would describe the relationship between resource variables such as per capita income or state revenue and the expenditure levels for various public services. As state wealth increases, the possibility of devoting ever greater funds to pollution control or tuition-free higher education also increases, but the growth in state wealth does not, in itself, assure that either change will take place. It is this failure to determine the minimum as well as the maximum output level that states will achieve that leads to the heteroscedasticity evident in Figure 3–3 and prevents the correlation between a necessary but not sufficient condition and the output from being high.

Education Continued

In addition to explaining why median education acting as a resource constraint cannot be expected to be highly correlated with de-institutionalization, the preceding discussion suggests that it is possible to test whether the demand or resource explanation more accurately characterizes the relationship between education and deinstitutionaliza-tion. If education has an impact on deinstitutionalization by being one of several factors capable of increasing the demand for innovative correc-tional programs (i.e., a sufficient but not necessary condition), we would expect the scatter plot of their relationship to resemble Figure 3–2. As the level of education increases, and supposedly with it the demand for innovation, the lower boundary of the plot should also increase.

Should median education function as a resource constraint, then the plot would resemble Figure 3–3. Because education would act as a neces-sary but not sufficient prerequisite for attaining a high level of deinstitutionalization, it would define the upper boundary of the plot but not the lower. Although the mean level of deinstitutionalization would rise as education increased, a number of states with high median educa-tion could have very low levels of deinstitutionalization.

The Impact of Delinquency, Income, Urbanization, Industrialization, and Education: Findings

The zero-order correlations of the two measures of delinquency and the four socioeconomic variables with deinstitutionalization are reported in Table 3–2. They are similar to what was anticipated, and strikingly

Table 3–2
Impact of Socioeconomic Variables

	Deinstitutionalization
Adjudicated delinquents per capita	.06
Property crime index	.10
Per capita income	.14
Urbanization	.07
Industrialization	−.18
Median education	.34

dissimilar (except in the case of education) from those in Table 3–1. As predicted, delinquency rate, per capita income, urbanization, and industrialization do not appear to function as significant exogenous parameters.

As for the relationship between education and deinstitutionalization, the scatter plot is shown in Figure 3–4 and one can see that the variance is markedly heteroscedastic. No state with a median education level lower than 11.98 years has achieved a deinstitutionalization rate of more than 17.5 percent. Fourteen states fall into this category. States with median education scores above 11.98 years exhibit a wide variation in their deinstitutionalization rates, although fourteen of them have rates no greater than the set of states with the low educational levels. This plot resembles Figure 3–3 much more closely than it does Figure 3–1 or 3–2. Education would appear to function as a *resource* constraint rather than a *demand* constraint: A certain amount of education appears necessary for extensive deinstitutionalization, but it is not sufficient to ensure that it will take place.

In addition to showing that certain socioeconomic characteristics that are traditionally thought to determine the nature of policy outputs do not invariably do so, these findings suggest that bureaucratically dominated policy outputs may be constrained by certain kinds of socioeconomic *resources*—in this instance the education level of the citizenry—more than they are influenced by socioeconomic *demands*, at least as measured by these crude indicators.

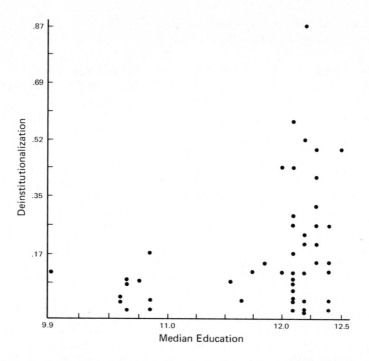

Figure 3–4. Scatter Plot: Deinstitutionalization-Median Education.

Additional Indicators/Determinants of Community
Tolerance and Receptivity

Obviously it is unwise to carry such speculations too far simply on the basis of the relationship between median education and deinstitutionaliza- tion. Single-item indicators possess a well-recognized capacity to mis- lead, especially when they are not securely linked to the concept of which they are believed to be indicative. While median education is one measure of community tolerance and receptivity in a state, it is hardly isomorphic with those dimensions—perhaps partly because they themselves are somewhat ambiguous. It is therefore desirable to examine other variables likely to be indicative of, and preferably determinants of as well, these public attitudes that are thought to constitute a necessary resource for the extensive adoption of deinstitutionalization.

One possible indicator of tolerance to deviancy and receptivity to innovative social programs is the liberality of the population. The per- centages of the vote received by Humphrey in 1968 and McGovern in

1972 were correlated with the dependent variable, with the expectation that they would both be positively related. Because of the greater erosion of traditional voting patterns in 1972 (particularly in the South), it was assumed that the average McGovern voter was considerably more liberal on domestic issues—including crime—than the average Humphrey voter. Not surprisingly then, the correlation between the Humphrey vote and deinstitutionalization was found to be .28, as compared to .47 for the McGovern vote.

An alternative indicator of the social and political philosophies that dominate a state's outlook is Elazar's [1966] classification of political cultures. On the basis of impressions gathered from published studies, state histories, the pronouncements of public officials, newspapers, voting data, and fieldwork, Elazar identified three distinct political cultures in the United States that he terms Moralist, Individualist, and Traditionalist. These cultures represent varying views toward political participation, bureaucracy, governmental intervention within the community, and the initiation of new programs. For example:

The Moralist culture welcomes the initiation of new programs for the good of the community; in the Individualistic culture, new programs would be initiated only if they could be described as political favors that would elicit favors in return for those who provided the programs; and the Traditionalist would accept new programs only if they were necessary for the maintenance of the status quo [Sharkansky, 1969:69].

We would hypothesize that Moralist cultures would be the most receptive to a correctional innovation like deinstitutionalization, Individualist cultures considerably less so, and Traditionalist cultures not at all. An individual with a Moralist perspective would be attracted to deinstitutionalization because it is believed to generate positive externalities for the entire state by reducing unnecessary expenditures and by increasing the possibility of rehabilitation. The Individualist would be cool to the innovation since community programs, because of their lower cost and fewer staff, involve substantially fewer patronage benefits.[h] Finally, the Traditionalist would be hostile to deinstitutionalization, because it involves redistributing offenders and money throughout the juvenile justice system, thereby bringing about a radical alteration of the status quo.

Sharkansky [1969] has taken Elazar's classification scheme and created a unidimensional index which ranges from Moralism to Indi-

---

[h]It is not unusual for large juvenile institutions to be the principal employers in certain rural communities and to have been placed (and maintained) there at least partly as a political favor.

vidualism to Traditionalism. He correlated the index with a wide variety of outputs and found it to be strongly related to "measures of service" (e.g., welfare expenditures), even after controlling for personal income and urbanization [Sharkansky, 1969:81]. The zero-order correlation between this index and deinstitutionalization is −.44, which provides additional evidence that community attitude is a significant determinant of correctional innovation.

At this point it is desirable to attempt to probe more deeply into the socioeconomic characteristics that might be responsible for, rather than merely indicative of, an atmosphere of public opinion favorable to correctional innovation. What, if anything, can be said about the socioeconomic prerequisites of that attitude? Do variations in state political culture and liberality have their roots in more fundamental socioeconomic explanations? Part of the answer to these questions may lie in state variations in median educational attainment, but there is another possible explanation.

Political analysts have long viewed the existence of social, cultural, and religious cleavages as dysfunctional to the development of public regardingness, the provision of public goods, and initiation of social programs in general [Lipset and Rokkan, 1967; Rokkan, 1968; Banfield and Wilson, 1963; Lineberry and Fowler, 1967; Aiken and Alford, 1970]. It seems only reasonable to expect that these cleavages would have an impact on a state's toleration of deviancy and acceptance of a social innovation such as deinstitutionalization. In states where class and racial divisions are deep, we would anticipate there to be a punitive approach to deviancy, particularly when deviants belong to a stratum of the population that does not have access to the reins of decision making. On the other hand, states in which the population is relatively homogeneous with respect to social class, income, and race would seem to contain an environment more conducive to the integration of delinquents into the community.

One of the two dimensions of social structure obtained by Cameron and Hofferbert et al. [1972:290] through factor analysis has been labeled "integration" and bears some resemblance to social and economic homogeneity. The correlation between integration and deinstitutionalization is .26. However, this integration factor is a mixture of elements such as affluence, higher education, and tertiary-sector economic development as well as racial and class cleavages [Cameron et al., 1975:24]. In order to explore the relationship between heterogeneity/homogeneity and the dependent variable somewhat more closely, a set of five variables that were thought to tap that dimension more directly were run against deinstitutionalization. The results are shown in Table 3–3.

Table 3–3
Relationship between Deinstitutionalization and Indicators of
Heterogeneity/Homogeneity

	Percent Black	Percent Nonwhite	GINI	Percent <125%[a]	Percent <5ED[b]	Composite[c]
Deinstitution-alization	−.33	−.30	−.32	−.25	−.42	−.39

[a]The percentage of adults whose income is less than 125 percent of the poverty line.
[b]The percentage of adults with less than five years of education.
[c]The composite index was created by adding the standardized scores of the other five variables.

These correlations provide modest but consistent support for the hypothesis that racial and class cleavages are negatively associated with our correctional innovation. Furthermore, the fact that the correlation between the percentage of the adult population with less than five years of education is more strongly related to the dependent variable than median education (−.42 versus .34) seems to imply that the uneven distribution of educational benefits may be more important than the absolute level.

The complete intercorrelation matrix of all the indicators and determinants of community tolerance and receptivity to social programs is reported in Table 3–4. A quick perusal indicates several items of interest. First, the measures of social heterogeneity are highly interrelated. When factor analyzed along with the other variables in the matrix, they load at .79 or above on an essentially one-dimensional solution that accounts for 66 percent of the total variance. Second, one could persuasively argue that political culture, as measured by Elazar, is primarily a manifestation of certain fundamental social and economic cleavages within the states. The correlation between political culture and the composite measure of heterogeneity is an impressive .82, which is by itself an interesting finding. Third, the McGovern and Humphrey votes, while definitely related to cleavages and heterogeneity, are not associated as strongly as political culture. It would seem that one aspect of the liberality of public opinion, at least as measured by these variables, cannot be explained solely on the existence or nonexistence of cleavages.

So far we have examined a fairly substantial amount of data that appears to corroborate the view that the attitudes of the citizenry are associated with the extent of deinstitutionalization. Perhaps more importantly, we have even made some progress toward fashioning a theory about the determinants of those attitudes. Now that we know something about the *magnitude* at which the various indicators and determinants of

Table 3–4
Intercorrelation Matrix of Indicators and Determinants of Community Tolerance and Receptivity to Social Programs

	Com-posite	% Black	% Nonwhite	% <125%	% <5ED	GINI	Median Ed.	Political Culture	% McGov	% Humphrey
Composite	1.00									
Percent black	.84	1.00								
Percent nonwhite	.77	.65	1.00							
Percent <125%	.79	.51	.33	1.00						
Percent <5ED	.94	.75	.70	.72	1.00					
GINI	.91	.67	.59	.80	.80	1.00				
Median education	-.79	-.69	-.41	-.72	-.79	-.74	1.00			
Political culture	.82	.78	.52	.64	.79	.77	-.72	1.00		
Percent vote McGovern	-.55	-.53	-.39	-.48	-.46	-.49	.39	-.61	1.00	
Percent vote Humphrey	-.60	-.60	-.27	-.61	-.47	-.58	.45	-.61	.72	1.00

state attitudes relate to the dependent variable, we must look at the *functional form* of the relationships. Do those variables that have been introduced since median education relate to deinstitutionalization in the same manner?

Figures 3–5 and 3–6 contain scatter plots of the relationships between deinstitutionalization and states' GINI indices (a measure of income inequality), as well as the percentage of the adult population with less than five years of education. Both are representative of the plots relating each of the socioeconomic variables in Table 3–4 to the dependent variable. As in the case of median education, the plots are extremely heteroscedastic and even more reminiscent of the plot anticipated from a necessary but not sufficient condition (i.e., Figure 3–3).[i] Whereas Figure 3–4 (containing median education) could be decomposed into two more or less

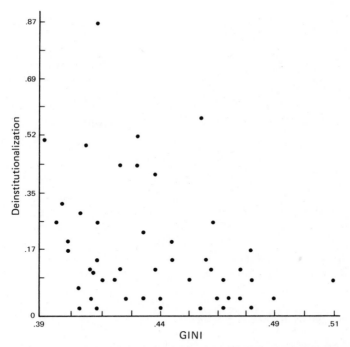

Figure 3–5. Scatter Plot: Deinstitutionalization-GINI Index.

---

[i]The only difference between Figure 3–3 and Figures 3–5 and 3–6 is that the latter are characterized by decreasing rather than increasing variance. This merely indicates that the signs of the relationships depicted are different.

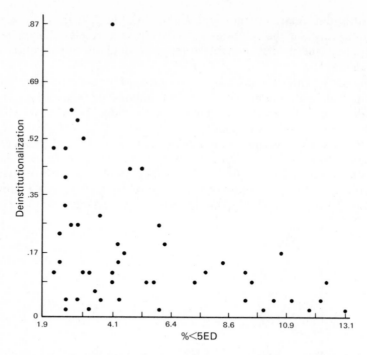

Figure 3–6. Scatter Plot: Deinstitutionalization-Percentage of Population with Less than Five Years Education.

distinct strata (i.e., states with education levels above and below 11.98), Figures 3–5 and 3–6 show a more gradual and constant increase in the upper boundary of the plots. Once again there is no lower boundary to either plot; a number of states with a fairly equitable distribution of income and only a small percentage of uneducated adults have, nonetheless, achieved no significant level of deinstitutionalization. These are precisely the plots we anticipate being generated by resource constraints.

Additional Socieconomic Variables

Table 3–5 contains a number of additional socioeconomic characteristics that might have been expected to be related to deinstitutionalization. The zero-order correlation between the dependent variable and each characteristic is listed. Only two (percent female-headed households and percent foreign stock) are even slightly related to deinstitutionalization, and both

Table 3–5
Additional Socioeconomic Variables and Correlation with
Deinstitutionalization

Total population	−.13
Percent population under 18	−.02
Unemployment rate (summer 1974)	.11
Percent female-headed households	−.28
Percent with over 4 years college	.05
Percent foreign stock	.35
Area	−.13
Population density	−.09
Percent population in central cities	−.11

are highly correlated (approximately .7 and above) with the set of variables measuring heterogeneity and political culture. Thus there is no indication that additional socioeconomic dimensions affect correctional innovation. Furthermore, we can still state that *every* socioeconomic variable correlated at .20 or higher relates to deinstitutionalization heteroscedastically in the manner of a necessary but not sufficient cause or resource constraint.

Conclusion

Typically in social science research it is much easier to summarize the results of data analysis than to discuss the theoretical implications of the findings, and this case is no exception. The former is a fairly straightforward process:

1. The majority of socioeconomic characteristics are unrelated to the dependent variable. These include urbanization, industrialization, and per capita income—the three variables that are the core of the unidimensional view of socioeconomic development and that customarily account for the bulk of the variance explained by both socioeconomic variables and all variables.
2. A number of socioeconomic indicators and determinants of states' probable tolerance of deviancy and receptivity toward innovative social programs were found to be related to deinstitutionalization. Specifically, liberality as indicated by two presidential elections, Elazar's index of political culture, and five indicators of social and economic heterogeneity are all correlated with the dependent variable at approximately .4.
3. The variables described immediately above all relate to the dependent variable in the manner of necessary but not sufficient conditions—

that is, they appear to determine the maximum—but not the minimum—extent of deinstitutionalization that will be attained by a state. This is the functional relationship that we associate with a resource constraint.

Most of the theoretical implications are not quite so clear-cut, except one that concerns the multidimensional character of the socioeconomic environment. These findings show quite conclusively that there are dimensions of that environment which are related to policy outputs but are uncorrelated with indicators of economic development. Had we employed only those variables (per capita income, urbanization, industrialization) supposed to tap the latter dimension, we would have been able to account for less than 5 percent of the variance in deinstitutionalization rates. As it was, we were able to account for 25 percent of the variance using measures of liberality and socioeconomic heterogeneity.

Beyond this point the implications are less clear but more provocative. One implication might be that the only socioeconomic characteristics affecting policy innovations in which the bureaucracy is intimately involved are those shaping social values. However, such a conclusion would seem precipitous. While it is probably true that the impact of certain socioeconomic characteristics (especially per capita income) on public policy in general and policy innovation in particular has been overestimated because of the type of outputs examined (e.g., expenditures) and the way they were measured (e.g., the date a policy innovation was adopted), it would almost certainly be a mistake to attempt to generalize too freely from these findings. Had we, for instance, been looking at a very costly social innovation such as a generous negative income tax, per capita income may well have proved to be a powerful determinant. It would seem wiser to conclude that state wealth and urbanization are not invariably related to policy outputs and may be quite irrelevant to a certain class—possibly large in size—of policy innovations that involve the redistribution of resources or the reordering of priorities.

Even more interesting from the point of view of understanding bureaucratic innovation is the finding that socioeconomic variables relate to deinstitutionalization in the manner of resource constraints. The implication that the socioeconomic environment is capable of restricting innovation by withholding necessary resources but incapable of assuring that it will take place by creating a high level of demand is certainly worthy of further investigation. Referring to the decomposability of the bureaucracy from its socioeconomic environment, we are left with the hypothesis that the bureaucracy may be decomposable on the demand side but not on the resource or supply side. This raises the possibility that bureaucracies may both ignore public pressure for innovation and, under favorable conditions, institute policies for which there is virtually no demand.

As a final point, it should be noted that these theoretical implications appear, in turn, to have several implications for research on policy determinants. One is that we have to begin thinking more rigorously about the magnitude and the functional form of the impact of particular socioeconomic variables and dimensions on outputs. For example, the sort of *reductio ad absurdum* arguments in which analysts postulate a situation in which there is no industrialization and therefore no need for industrial pollution control standards and then jump to the conclusion that there must be a strong relationship between the two should be held to a minimum.

Furthermore, it would seem wise to check the functional form of relationships before believing that the correlation or regression coefficient is an accurate reflection of the association between a determinant and an output. In this case it was one thing to say that the correlation between median education and the dependent variable is .34 and another to say that no state with an education level below 11.98 attained a deinstitutionalization score above the mean. Whether or not we are aware of the second piece of information will have much to do with our estimate of the "importance" of a variable.

4

The Impact of the Task Environment

This chapter deals with the composition, characteristics, and impact of the more immediate and nonsocioeconomic environment of juvenile corrections bureaucracies. This portion of the environment has been variously termed the "task environment" [Dill, 1958; Thompson 1967], the organization's "market," the "external selection environment" [Friedman, 1974; Nelson and Winter, 1975], and the "organization set" [Evan, 1966]. It can be loosely defined as those organizations and institutions in the focal organization's environment that are relevant to goal setting and attainment [Thompson, 1967:28]. As we have seen, little quantitative research has been conducted in this area by either determinants or innovation researchers, and it has only been relatively recently that organizational theorists have even begun to initiate empirical work on organizational environments [Lawrence and Lorsch, 1970; Duncan, 1971].

This is not to imply that *no* research has been carried out on the manner and extent to which elements in an organization's or institution's environment affect its structure and outputs. Such matters have frequently been the focal point of case studies, from Selznick's classic *TVA and the Grass Roots* [1949] to Friedman's research on correctional innovations [1973]. Studies conducted by political scientists, many of which deal with the task environment of legislatures [e.g., Bauer, Pool, and Dexter, 1963], are well known and numerous.

Cumulatively these studies have led to a general appreciation of the variety of ways in which environmental elements can affect organizations through the control of resources and the manipulation of various kinds of constraints. However, individually they have also possessed the inevitable drawbacks of all case studies: the unclear specification of dimensions, the inability to make precise statements about the impact of individual variables, and the difficulties involved in appropriately qualifying generalizations. In a sense, what follows can be seen partly as an attempt to explore many of the issues dealt with in traditional case studies within a comparative, quantitative framework, which although crudely exploratory and plagued by its own limitations, appears to be a logical step forward.

As stated in Chapter 2, the formal integration of environmental elements into the decision-making process of public sector organizations is commonplace, and correctional bureaucracies are no exception. Legislatures must appropriate their funds and not uncommonly must agree to major programmatic changes before they can be implemented. Governors and their staffs must approve budget recommendations and similarly must pass on major policy innovations. They also frequently play a major role in the selection of key personnel, as do unions and civil service systems, which can hinder the ability of agency directors to make a variety of crucial personnel decisions. In several states judges have the power to commit offenders directly to particular programs and must approve all applications for transfer or release.

Environmental units can potentially play a role in determining the goals and priorities of the bureaucracy as well as affecting their attainment. Often this process is very obvious and formalized, as in the case where the director of a cabinet-level "umbrella" agency (e.g., state department of human resources) must give final approval to an explicit set of correctional-agency priorities. Sometimes it is indirect and somewhat more subtle, as in the case of professional groups that are in a position to confer prestige on agency professionals who behave in what the groups consider to be an exemplary fashion.

In comparison with the markets of private sector organizations one cannot help but be struck by the *extent* to which external elements are *formally* integrated into a correctional agency's decision-making process. Decisions that in the private sector would be made internally in each firm—in spite of the expanding role of the government in the private sector as a simultaneous consumer and regulator—are frequently collective decisions for these agencies that must get judges, governors, and key legislative committee persons to "go along" formally. This would seem to argue for the importance of identifying the priorities of environmental elements with the expectation that they will play a major role in determining the policies of the bureaucracy. However, this assumes that such elements are both able and inclined to form independent positions (i.e., independent from those which the bureaucracy advocates) on the various issues under consideration. Here it is useful to recall that a number of scholars, such as Rourke [1969], Lowi [1969], and Salisbury and Heinz [1973], have pointed to the widespread de facto delegation of policy-making authority to bureaucracies.

During the case-study phase of this research we identified and interviewed the leaders and spokespersons of organizations and institutions that actively and consistently worked to have an impact on state juvenile corrections policy. This preliminary research resulted in, among other things, the identification of eight principal categories of external actors in the policy process:

1. Legislature—especially floor leaders, key committee persons and committee staff;

2. Governor and staff;
3. Judges and court administrators;
4. Interest groups (e.g., League of Women Voters, ACLU);
5. State Planning Agency (a federally mandated, criminal justice planning agency whose existence is a prerequisite for the receipt of federal funds);
6. Other state agencies (e.g., welfare department, mental health);
7. Professional associations (e.g., American Bar Association, National Association of Social Workers);
8. Employee unions.

This list became the basis for a number of questions administered in all fifty states about agency-environment relations. These revealed a number of interesting results even at a descriptive level. For instance, while the composition of this list is no great surprise, the amount of cross-state variation in the activities of these groups is not widely recognized. Although juvenile corrections agency executives are generally aware of the many problems and concerns they share with their colleagues, there are some pronounced differences in the worlds in which they must work. Eight state executives found themselves regularly dealing with *ten or more* state-level interest groups, while in five states *not a single* interest group was active in the area of juvenile corrections. In nine states the executives met with staff personnel from the governor's office *three or more times a week,* while thirteen state executives met with such staff *less than once per month.* This same sort of variation existed with respect to contact with legislators (even controlling for length of session), courts, and other agencies. Similarly, the priorities of these groups differed considerably and their interest and participation in the area varied enormously. Such variation raises the possibility that a wide range of environmental dimensions or market characteristics may be responsible for output variation in general and differing deinstitutionalization rates in particular. Not only might variation in the priorities of environmental elements have an impact on bureaucratic behavior, but so also might differences in the frequency of contact between the agency and the environment, the heterogeneity of the environment, its instability, the integration of external demands, etc.

Political Variables

Before exploring the impact of the task environment in the manner of an organization theorist or someone conducting a case study, the tradition of comparative state policy analysis would seem to demand that we examine the "effect" of certain political variables on state deinstitutionalization rates. The policy innovation we are attempting to account for is a nonfiscal output of the sort most critics of classic determinants studies believe are determined by political variables independently of socioeconomic ones.

Previous analyses of policy outcomes have generally indicated that socioeconomic variables have a dominant influence on these outcomes, with few reported instances of political variables exerting an independent impact. We have contended that these results have been the product of a continuing concentration on policy outcomes as measured by levels of taxes and expenditures [Fry and Winters, 1970:521].

We believe this simply outrageous description of state politics is an artifact of inadequate measurement of concepts, the utilization of inappropriate techniques of analysis, and overly narrow definitions of what constitutes politically relevant outputs and outcomes [Jacob and Vines 1971:558].

Not only is deinstitutionalization a nonfiscal output, it is an output that varies almost completely independently of the socioeconomic variables that usually account for the bulk of the explained variance in expenditure outputs. Thus it appears to provide a favorable set of circumstances for revealing the long-awaited independent impact of such political variables as legislative professionalism and malapportionment. On the other hand, if these political variables are related to policy only when the socioeconomic environment is, which implies a spurious relation between the political variables and outputs—the independence of deinstitutionalization from most socioeconomic variables may also foreshadow an independence from political variables.

Certainly it is difficult not to possess some reservations to the unqualified expectation that the political variables commonly employed will have a significant impact on deinstitutionalization rates simply because the "basic" socioeconomic variables do not. Merely establishing independence between socioeconomic variables and an output, either theoretically or empirically, is hardly tantamount to demonstrating that a few political variables "matter." Variation in other, considerably more complex political dimensions may be responsible for the differing deinstitutionalization rates, or it is possible that the universe of political variables are only marginally relevant. If, as many scholars contend, the bureaucracy has assumed extensive unilateral policy-making powers, the latter situation may in fact exist, in which case we would expect that correlations generated by political variables would be either small or spurious.

The results of previous studies that have employed nonfiscal output measures are equivocal on the issue of the extent of independent association between political variables and these outputs. Both Booms and Halldorson [1973] and Fry and Winters [1970] found several moderate zero-order and partial correlations (controlling for socioeconomic variables) between their respective redistribution indices and political variables (specifically, legislative professionalism and voter turnout). Nonetheless, the majority of political variables in both studies had only a negligible effect. Walker [1969] looked at a number of political variables (malapportionment, party competition, turnover in office, and legislative professionalism), but although the zero-order correlations ranged from .26 to .65, all the relationships declined dramatically when controls were introduced for socioeconomic variables, with the single exception of malapportionment. LeMay's [1973] study of the determinants of legislative activity in the area of urban problems also produced significant zero-order betas between political variables and his output measure, which eroded completely when socioeconomic variables were introduced into the regression equation. While not entirely contradicting the expectations of the critics of determinants studies, such results have been much less positive in revealing the independent impact of political variables than was hoped.

The zero-order correlations between ten characteristics of state political systems and deinstitutionalization are presented in Table 4–1. Except for that involving the competition/turnout factor, these correlations are strikingly low, despite the fact that no socioeconomic variables have been introduced as control variables. Realizing that an argument could be made about the inappropriateness of investigating the impact of party while including the southern states, these states were taken out of the analysis

Table 4–1
Political Variable Correlations

	All States	Nonsouthern States
Competition/turnout factor score [Sharkansky and Hofferbert 1969]	.30	.11
Legislative professionalism [Sharkansky and Hofferbert 1969]	.04	.00
Governor's power [Schlesinger 1965]	.19	.10
Interest-group politics [Zeller 1954]	−.14	.01
Malapportionment [Schubert and Press 1964]	−.04	.01
Party of governor[a]	.04	.05
Senate party[a]	−.04	−.20
House party[a]	.04	−.13
Total party[a]	.02	−.17

[a] A positive correlation signifies an association between Republican domination and the dependent variable, a negative correlation the reverse.

and the correlations rerun. The results, however, did not change appreciably (see Table 4–1). Although the exclusion of the southern states did result in an increase in the association between Democratic control and deinstitutionalization, the increase is not substantial.

As for the correlation of .30 generated by the Sharkansky-Hofferbert competition/turnout factor, it behaves in a manner typical of other relationships between political characteristics and policy outputs—that is, it disappears when socioeconomic variables are included in the analysis. In this case, however, the socioeconomic variable that produced this effect is not urbanization or per capita income but rather any of the measures of heterogeneity considered in the previous chapter. The composite indicator of heterogeneity is correlated with competition/turnout at $-.82$. When they are inserted together in a regression equation, their respective beta weights are $-.42$ for heterogeneity and $-.05$ for competition/turnout. These results plus the partial correlations show that competition/turnout may function to a *very* small extent as an intervening variable but that for the most part its impact is spurious. There is no evidence that it has any independent impact.

Granted that these political variables appear to have no general impact, do they have a conditional one? Do these variables interact with others? Perhaps legislative professionalism has a significant effect on deinstitutionalization only when the autonomy of the correctional agency is restricted by constitutional provision necessitating that it work closely with the legislature. Or perhaps its impact is affected by the legislature's traditional level of participation in correctional policy making.

Hypotheses like these were tested for each political variable by looking at their correlations with deinstitutionalization after stratifying the states on the basis of the traditional participation of the relevant group (legislature, governor, etc.) in policy making and the decision-making autonomy of the agency. This exercise did reveal conditional impacts (which for the most part were in the direction expected); however, the resultant correlations were invariably small. For instance, in those states where the legislature has not participated in policy making and has traditionally shown little interest in corrections,[a] the correlation generated by legislative professionalism is $-.26$, while among those states in which the legislature is active the correlation is $+.25$. This is close to what we would have expected, but the magnitude of the within-stratum correlations is much too small (especially considering the Ns) to be theoretically interesting.[b]

---

[a] As perceived by the correctional agency executive.

[b] Actually, while we would have expected the r to increase in the second stratum, there is no reason to anticipate that it would be negative in the first stratum.

What else are we to conclude from this almost perfect lack of association between these political variables and the dependent variable? It is clear that these results alone do not provide conclusive evidence that legislators and governors have no effect on policy outputs, even in this single case. Obviously there are numerous dimensions of state political systems and the behavior of their elements that are not subsumed by this handful of variables. Yet it would also be inappropriate to dismiss the findings by arguing that these variables are inadequate, simplistic indicators of political structure and activity. To do so would be to disregard the fact that these same variables have previously been shown to represent some portion of the linkage between socioeconomic development and certain outputs [Cnudde and McCrone, 1969]. Perhaps the most appropriate conclusion is simply to state that the findings reported here are consistent with those of the many studies that have found that a number of theoretically meaningful political variables only affect outputs when certain socioeconomic variables do. In this case, of course, neither set of variables had any impact.

Thus, this research provides a counterexample to the findings of Fry and Winters [1970] and Booms and Halldorson [1973] that appear to support the contention of many political scientists that political variables have an independent impact on nonfiscal outputs, even if they have little impact on expenditure levels. Just how these two sets of findings might be reconciled will be discussed in the concluding chapter, but one possibility is that political variables may have a significant impact only on those nonfiscal outputs that are politically salient. This would explain why legislative professionalism and malapportionment are more closely related to variations in state redistribution rates than to deinstitutionalization rates.

The Priorities of Environmental Units

Perhaps a more logical point at which to have begun an exploration of the impact of the bureaucracy's task environment on its policy decisions is with the priorities, both individual and collective, of the elements of which it is composed. Just as the requirements and desires of the airlines and FAA determine to some extent the kind of innovations Boeing adopts [Nelson and Winter, 1975], so we anticipate the priorities of the governor's office, the legislature, the courts, and other agencies, to have an impact on the behavior (innovative and otherwise) of a state corrections agency. These groups simultaneously constitute, in a very real sense, the consumers, suppliers, and regulators of agency outputs. And, according to studies such as Friedman's [1974], the values and priorities of these groups determine the "worth" of an innovation in the same way their private sector counterparts determine what is profitable.

However, as the introductory section of this chapter implied, there are at least two lines of argument appearing in the literature that lead to conflicting expectations about the congruence between environmental goals and agency outputs. Both positions emphasize the ambiguous and uncertain outcomes of many public sector innovations. In addition, the first stresses the collective decision process that presents elements in the environment with the power and the opportunity to press for the policies most beneficial to them and their constituents. The uncertainty of outcomes attached to any particular policy position permits them to do this without fear of authoritative contradiction. Thus a situation arises where the parameters of the solution to many public sector problems are unknown or objectively undefinable (in a welfare economic sense) and elements in the environment are empowered—de jure if not de facto—to define them in a manner optimal to them. Friedman's study is filled with examples of how units in the selection or evaluation environment were able to mold two nonbureaucratic correctional innovations to their own ends because they possessed a power to do so which was unchecked by any certainty about the benefit-cost configuration involved in their positions.

The opposing position does not take issue with the potential ability of various environmental units to influence bureaucratic policy outputs but contends that most lack the incentive to do so. The causes of this absence of incentives are several. Groups in the environment may feel that to explore possible policy positions and bargain with other groups is too costly (in both staff time and money) in comparison with the benefits they are likely to accrue [Salisbury and Heinz, 1969]. This point emphasizes the "marginality" [Vinter, 1974] of many public sector decisions to the groups that are in a position to influence them. The outcomes of these decisions may simply not be that important to them.

The situation can also arise where the outcome of a particular policy alternative or innovation is so uncertain that the environmental unit cannot confidently begin to evaluate it no matter how much access to expertise it might have. The decision may matter a great deal, but because the environmental group has no basis upon which to make a decision (i.e., no way of knowing which outcome will benefit it), it abdicates its decision-making authority. In this case it is the *obscurity* of the benefit-cost ratio attached to alternatives rather than their magnitude that leads groups to defer to the bureaucracy.

It is not difficult to argue that deinstitutionalization may be one of those policies that does not provide environmental elements with strong incentives to intercede for or against it. The level of funding involved is nothing compared to the sums spent by states on mental health, education, or welfare; nor can legislatures and governors confidently predict the outcomes of pursuing a policy of deinstitutionalization in terms of cost, recidivism, or life chances.

Preliminary field research in the sixteen states revealed a situation that tends to support the second line of reasoning. This research indicated that there was a great amount of variability in the interest of environmental elements in the area of juvenile corrections. Not infrequently groups were very active, and their interest was often motivated by a strong ideological stance. However, they rarely expressed any strong preferences regarding specific policy alternatives—primarily because the consequences of engaging in any given course of action were so obscure.[c] Often groups realized that something should be done but did not know what the something should be and found it quite difficult to translate their general ideological position into programmatic terms. Thus there was some support for the expectation that the correlations between environmental priorities and deinstitutionalization would not be high.

Extensive interviews with judges, legislators, governors' staffs, interest-group representatives, and others, during the case-study phase of the research uncovered seven goals of varying specificity that were mentioned more often than others:

1. Cost reduction (abbreviated *Cost*);
2. Community protection (*Protect*);
3. Reduction of institutional population (*Reduce*);
4. Development of community-based corrections (*Com. Base*);
5. The diversion of greater resources to juvenile corrections (*Resource*);
6. The protection of the rights of juvenile offenders (*Rights*);
7. The upgrading of vocational and treatment programs in institutions (*Upgrade*).

The seven priorities constitute the basis of a simplified model of the complex pattern of demands that comprise the external selection environment of juvenile corrections.

After satisfying ourselves during this same phase of research that the perceptions of correctional administrators reliably characterized the priorities of environmental elements,[d] the directors of the agency given primary responsibility for the operation of juvenile corrections were

---

[c]This tended to be truer of legislators, executive staff, and some judges than of interest-group representatives, although even they quite frequently had no strong programmatic priorities.

[d]The congruence between the executive's perceptions and the acknowledged priorities of environmental group representatives permits us to finesse the interesting question of whether, in fact, their goals as *perceived* by the executive or their *actual* ones should be used in the analysis.

asked to assign the priority given these goals by the five principal environmental groups: the legislature and its staff, the governor and his staff, judges and court administrators, interest groups, and the state planning agency. Obviously this required a great deal of simplification on the part of the respondent; not all interest groups or all judges pull in the same direction. However, it was believed that the relative simplicity of the "politics of corrections" would prevent any great distortion of reality. Fortunately, in the vast majority of states it proved possible to characterize the priorities of interest groups as a whole with little or no difficulty and administrators were able to do so quite easily.

Like most policy issues that arise in juvenile corrections, deinstitutionalization involves a number of these goals. It was anticipated that a commitment to priorities 3 (Reduce) and 4 (Com. Base) would act to encourage a policy of deinstitutionalization, while a commitment to 2 (Protect) and 7 (Upgrade) would lead groups to oppose it. Priorities 5 (Resource) and 6 (Rights) were listed in order to investigate other policy outputs and will henceforth be omitted. As we have seen, the reduction of institutional populations (#3) and the establishment of community-based programs (#4) are the two methods by which the innovation is accomplished. On the negative side, the specter of decreased community protection is perhaps the principal argument used to oppose it. The rationale behind expecting a negative correlation between deinstitutionalization and a commitment to upgrading institutional treatment is somewhat less straightforward but basically quite simple. It was believed that this tactic would primarily be advocated by relatively conservative and traditional reform forces who saw imperfections in the status quo but responded to these imperfections in much the same way they did in the 1950s and 1960s—that is, by seeking to improve rather than discard juvenile institutions.

Despite the salience of cost reduction (#1), no specific expectation was formulated during the case study phase about how this priority would be related to the dependent variable. This uncertainty prevailed because although proponents of deinstitutionalization argued that it would eventually reduce costs, it was nonetheless common to request a budget increase for the purpose of initiating community-based programs. This presented environmental elements with something of a dilemma, and many expressed doubt and indecision about what the cost consequences of the innovation would be. This made it unclear whether, across the fifty states, environmental pressure to cut or limit spending would lead toward or away from a policy of deinstitutionalization.

Table 4–2 presents the zero-order correlations between the priorities of each group and state deinstitutionalization rates. Generally the results are in line with what was anticipated. Emphasis on the part of environ-

Table 4–2
Correlations between Environmental Priorities and Deinstitutionalization

Goal	Legislature	Governor's Office	Courts	Interest Groups	SPA
Cost	−.24	−.22	no variance	.05	.02
Protect	−.21	−.18	.19	−.02	.03
Reduce	.29	.15	no variance	.17	.07
Com. Base	.12	.29	.22	−.08	−.06
Upgrade	.13	−.03	−.24	−.18	−.21

mental groups on community protection and the upgrading of treatment is usually connected with less deinstitutionalization. On the other hand, the more groups value the development of community-based programs and the reduction of institutional populations, the more deinstitutionalization is likely to have taken place in their states. Legislative and gubernatorial interest in cost reduction turned out to be negatively related to the degree of innovation.

An interesting (and reassuring, from the perspective of validity) feature of the table is that the magnitude of the correlations declines as we move from the groups likely to have the greatest impact on legislation dealing with deinstitutionalization to those likely to have the least—that is, most of the correlations become smaller as we proceed from the legislature and the governor's office to the courts, then to interest groups and, lastly, to the state planning agency. Of course, in general the overall magnitudes of those relationships are not particularly great, although several are large enough to be of interest—especially when one considers the crudeness of the indicators.

Having attained some confidence that these priorities are related to the dependent variable in the manner hypothesized, it is appropriate to combine the individual priorities into collective ones. The rationale behind creating indicators of collective priorities stems from the belief that bureaucracies respond to the *total* amount of environmental pressure and that while the correlations generated by the priorities of individual elements may indicate which are the most influential (or the most *influenced* by the bureaucracy), they are likely to be attenuated by the priorities of other groups.

Table 4–3 contains the correlations between simple additive measures of the total emphasis placed on each of the five priorities by all five groups and the dependent variable.[e] Beyond the fact that they are all in

---

[e]It is reasonable to question the appropriateness of assigning the priorities of each group the same weight when it is obvious that they are unlikely to be equally influential. The only reply is that a variety of different weighting schemes were experimented with (based on perceived influence, amount of activity, etc.), but they did not improve results.

Table 4–3
Correlations between Collective Priorities and Deinstitutionalization

	Cost	Protect	Reduce	Com. Base	Upgrade	Composite
Deinst.	−.19	−.06	.08	.15	−.16	.27

the predicted direction, these correlations are too small to be especially enlightening. However, if it is reasonable to believe that the impact of the priorities of a single group is dependent on or cumulative with the priorities of other groups, it is just as reasonable to believe that the impact of any particular priority is likely to be influenced by other priorities.

With this in mind, another variable was constructed by subtracting the scores on those priorities that are negatively related to the dependent variable from those of the two that are positively related. The result is a single summary measure of environmental pressure for deinstitutionalization. Because it is sensitive to the amount of environmental-group consensus it is also a measure of what Salisbury and Heinz [1969] would call the "integration of demand" for that innovation. The correlation between this index and the dependent variable is .27, not particularly large but an improvement over virtually all of the correlations obtained by other measures of priorities, and more readily interpretable.

Before leaving the topic of environmental priorities, two categories of questions require further attention. First, how is the impact of these priorities tied to variability in the socioeconomic environment? Do they function as intervening variables; is their impact independent; does the introduction of socioeconomic variables indicate that their relationship to the dependent variable is spurious? Second, to what extent do they appear to reflect the priorities of the bureaucracy? The latter raises the methodologically slippery issue of which way the causal arrow points. Does the bureaucracy determine the priorities of the environment, or vice versa?

The correlation between the composite priority variable and the composite measure of heterogeneity constructed in the last chapter is −.37, which suggests that to at least a modest extent the socioeconomic environment influences the priorities of groups in the environment. In addition, when both are introduced in a multiple regression equation their respective betas are .14 and −.33, which indicates that a significant portion of the zero-order correlation between the priority variable and deinstitutionalization is due to the impact of heterogeneity on both (i.e., it is partially spurious).

The question concerning the extent to which environmental elements are influenced by the bureaucracy is an important one since many of the authors cited have stressed the ability of the bureaucracy to mold the opinions and perceptions of public officials and even interest groups. The only light that this data set is capable of shedding on this methodologically complex issue comes from the correlations between the priorities of the executive who runs the juvenile corrections agency and those of environmental groups. Executives were asked two sets of questions that probed the nature of their priorities and goals. One set was directed toward their ideal priorities, and the other toward those priorities that various constraints forced them to adopt. The correlations between the executives' ideal priorities and those of environmental groups were quite small and ranged (for the most part) from ±.05 to ±.20; those between the executives' constrained priorities and the priorities of environmental elements, which were slightly higher, ranged from ±.15 to ±.30. Clearly the size of the correlations furnishes some evidence that the bureaucracy is not "determining" the priorities of external groups (as well as vice versa, of course). In addition, the fact that the second set of relationships are stronger than the first suggests that the small association that does exist is caused by environmental priorities flowing toward the bureaucracy rather than the other way around.

Environmental "Interest" as a Resource

Aside from the relatively small impact of their priorities on agency outputs, a predictable consequence of the rarity of strong opinions held by environmental groups about specific policy alternatives was that agency executives were commonly much more concerned about the *indifference* of those groups than with their opposition. As a rule, the probability that legislation enabling the corrections agency to either initiate or increase community programs would die in committee for lack of support, or be passed but later casually chopped off in a general budget cut, was many times greater than the probability that it would be intentionally killed by opponents.

This problem of getting groups interested enough to ensure passage of key legislation often arose during our interviews with agency executives and others. The creation and maintenance of "visibility" for juvenile corrections is a continuing and time-consuming task, especially for those executives who desire that some sort of change take place.

In a complex series of questions, agency executives were asked to estimate the amount of influence environmental groups had had on juvenile corrections policy in the past few years. While it was originally thought that their responses would indicate the extent to which these groups determined the *direction* of policy, it quickly became apparent that executives were responding by providing the extent to which groups were *interested* and *active* in juvenile corrections policy making. This is no impressionistic inference: Executives consistently and invariably told interviewers that this was the basis for their answers. The reason they gave for this follows from what has been noted above—that is, environmental groups have an impact on juvenile corrections policy not by placing innovative proposals on the agenda of the legislature or by advocating a program-specific package of policies but by helping to ensure that the field maintains a degree of *visibility*, which in turn helps to ensure that a "fair share" of funds will be allocated, and that bureaucratically initiated proposals will be paid attention to.

Table 4–4 contains the correlations between deinstitutionalization and the amount of interest each of the five principal groups has

Table 4–4
The Impact of Environmental Activity/Interest

	Legislature	Governor's Office	Courts	Interest Groups	SPA	Composite
Deinstitution- alization	.44	.35	.27	.23	.21	.45

exhibited—or how "active" each has been—in the field of juvenile corrections (as perceived by the chief administrator of the bureaucracy). A composite measure of the interest across all these groups is also included for the same reason that a similar measure was included in the previous section.

Not only is each correlation in the appropriate direction, but the magnitudes of several—including the composite measure—are refreshingly substantial. It appears that active participation by environmental elements in juvenile corrections policy making significantly increases the probability that deinstitutionalization will take place.

Up to this point little has been said about the functional form of the relationships between task environment variables and deinstitutionalization. The reason for this is that the scatter plots created by the political and priority variables reveal neither inordinate heteroscedasticity nor potential nonlinearity. However, this is not true of the interest/activity measures. Figures 4–1 and 4–2 contain the plots of deinstitutionalization against the activity levels of the legislature and governor's office.

The functional form of both relationships are remarkably reminiscent of those between measures of socioeconomic heterogeneity and are similarly indicative (perhaps even more so) of a necessary but not sufficient

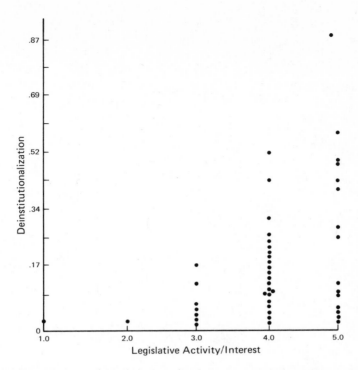

Figure 4–1. Scatter Plot: Deinstitutionalization-Legislative Activity/ Interest.

relationship. Like heterogeneity, the activity level of environmental groups appears to function as a resource constraint rather than as a demand. While the mean level of deinstitutionalization rises somewhat as the amount of legislative or gubernatorial activity increases, a substantial number of states at each level of activity have achieved no noticeable amount of deinstitutionalization. On the other hand, the upper bounds of the plots are quite clearly defined and rarely exceed a clearly defined threshold until a higher level of activity is reached.

Once again the functional form of the relationship permits us to make a tentative choice between a demand and a resource-constraint explanation. Had we been able to look only at the correlations, a quite plausible explanation of what was occurring would be that increasing activity and interest on the part of environmental groups forces the bureaucracy to grope for innovative solutions to what is universally recognized as being an unsatisfactory state of affairs. The scatter plots, however, argue against such a purely demand explanation unless one can demonstrate

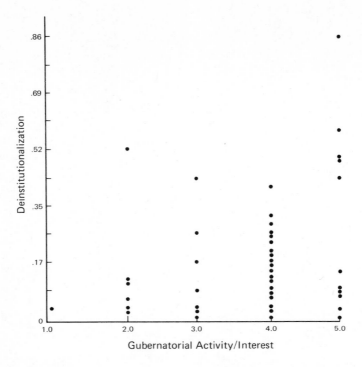

Figure 4–2. Scatter Plot: Deinstitutionalization-Gubernatorial Activity/
Interest.

that those states in which there are higher amounts of environmental
activity contain bureaucracies that are somehow insulated from their
environment in some special way. Yet if we stratify the states on the most
obvious indicator of bureaucratic insulation from the environment—that
is, the decision-making autonomy of the agency—there is no difference in
the within-stratum correlations between environmental activity and
deinstitutionalization (the r's = .27 and .29).

What is particularly interesting about the activity variables is that
they are *not* associated with measures of socioeconomic heterogeneity (or
any other socioeconomic dimensions, for that matter). The correlation
between the composite activity and heterogeneity indicator is only −.08,
and this is representative of all the correlations between heterogeneity
and the interest/activity of each group. Thus, whereas the priorities of
environmental groups were significantly related to heterogeneity (at
−.37), their level of participation in the field of juvenile corrections is not.

But if environmental activity is independent of the socioeconomic environment, is it also independent of the bureaucracy? What can be said about the issue of whether this dimension is wholly an *independent* resource or whether it is something that can be created and manipulated by the bureaucracy? After all, reference has already been made to the significant portion of time spent by correctional agency officials—especially the more dynamic ones—in drumming up interest among legislators, interest groups, and other elements in the environment. This indicates that there is at least an attempt on the part of the bureaucracy to control the level of environmental-group interest.

In a section of the interview schedule that asked about the frequency of contact between environmental groups and the upper echelons of the corrections agency, the executive was also asked whether the majority of those contacts were initiated by the outside group, the agency, or whether they each initiated about half of the contacts. If the agency were capable of influencing environmental interest/activity, we might expect that this activity would increase as the propensity of the agency to initiate the contacts increased, since the latter is likely to be an indicator of the extent to which the bureaucracy tries to manipulate its environment. The correlations between these crude three-category indicators of contact initiation and environmental-group interest/activity were all in the hypothesized direction and averaged about .20. This leads us to suspect that action on the part of the bureaucracy is slightly associated with the stimulation of environmental interest. However, the size of these correlations and the additional fact that correlations between executive priorities (ideal and constrained) and environmental interest are also small[f] suggest that the bulk of this interest is not created by the agency.

Additional Dimensions of the Task Environment

Up to this point the dimensions of the task environment that have been examined have been either political ones traditionally analyzed by determinants researchers or those which have intermittently been treated in a more or less impressionistic way by sociologists and political scientists engaged in case studies. In this section we turn to the three characteristics of the task environment most commonly hypothesized by organization theorists to be related to innovation.

---

[f]If executives could manipulate the level of environmental interest at will, we would anticipate that in those states where executives are very much against the status quo and in favor of deinstitutionalization, these executives would have increased the level of environmental activity in order to facilitate change.

Environmental Heterogeneity

Numerous authors [Wilson, 1966; Hage and Aiken, 1967; Baldridge and Burnham, 1975] have postulated that a positive relationship exists between the number of environmental elements with which an organization deals and its level of innovativeness. The logic behind this is based on the belief that as the heterogeneity of the environment or number of environmental groups increases, the organization is exposed to a greater number of innovative ideas and has more information to use as a basis for their evaluation. Environmental heterogeneity, like frequency of environmental contact that follows, is thought to result in an increase in the organizational equivalent of "cosmopoliteness," which is one of the most analyzed dimensions in social-psychological innovation research.

An indicator of heterogeneity was constructed by assigning each state a score based on the number of environmental elements that the executive said had at least some influence (i.e., interest) in juvenile corrections. Scores ranged from 0 in states with no active elements to 8 in states where every environmental group was at least moderately active. The correlation between this measure of heterogeneity and deinstitutionalization was .16, which is in the hypothesized direction but insubstantial.

Frequency of Environmental Contact

The rationale for expecting a positive relationship between the frequency of environmental contact and innovation is virtually identical to that concerning heterogeneity. The number of contacts per month between each environmental group and the corrections executive and his immediate assistants were added together and this score was correlated with the dependent variable. The resultant correlation was .08, which is again in the predicted direction but negligible in magnitude.

Environmental Instability

Through the work of Burns and Stalker [1961], Emery and Trist [1965], Terreberry [1968], and Duncan [1971], environmental instability, together with uncertainty, has become one of the most studied and discussed dimensions of the organizational environment. It too is believed to be positively related to innovation [Rogers, 1962; Zaltman et al., 1973], since it is thought to force organizations to rapidly adapt (i.e., innovate) in order to meet changing demands. The problems involved in selecting a satisfactory indicator (or set of indicators) of environmental variability are substantial, especially in such a comparative, exploratory study where there are no guidelines as to what sort of instability is likely to affect bureaucratic behavior. Two likely indicators of environmental variability were selected and correlated with deinstitutionalization:

1. *Number of administrative reorganizations.* Reorganizations of the state bureaucracy, by bringing about the realignment of traditional power relationships among agencies, channels of communication, and so forth can alter the nature of the corrections agency's task environment substantially. For instance, a reorganization may reduce the agency from a cabinet-level position and relocate it within a large, multifunction department of human resources that places its director under several noncorrections-oriented bureaucrats and limits his or her access to both legislators and the governor.[g] Furthermore, reorganizations are also likelier to take place when the state has undergone a major change (e.g., the election of a new governor) or major crisis (e.g., welfare scandal, prison or mental health exposé). The correlation between the number of reorganizations that have taken place in the past five years and deinstitutionalization is .32.

2. *Media criticism.* Frequent criticism from the press is often indicative of a certain amount of environmental volatility for a government agency (e.g., the CIA and EPA). Executives were asked to estimate the number of times in the previous two years that the juvenile justice system had come under attack by a major newspaper. The frequency of newspaper criticism is barely correlated with the dependent variable, at .03.

Of the three environmental dimensions believed by organization theorists to be related to innovation, only instability has produced a correlation of any significance. However, despite the evidence in favor of the hypothesis that environmental variability leads to innovation, one might question whether the *process* taking place here is identical to that usually described in the literature. Environmental variability is supposed to lead to innovation by necessitating new responses to changing situations, and sets of demands. But from what we know about the uncertainty regarding programmatic priorities that is characteristic of most environmental groups in corrections, it seems unlikely that changes in the task environment (e.g., election of a new governor, change in party control of the legislature, statewide administrative reorganization) would result in the agency having to face a radically different pattern of demands.

Yet, if reorganization does not expose the agency to shifting demand patterns, what is the process by which it leads to innovation? No entirely

---

[g]In at least two states reorganization has resulted in statutory limitations being placed on the right of the agency director to contact legislators; in still other states such reorganizations have resulted in similar de facto limitations.

satisfactory explanation is available, but part of the answer may be that reorganization increases the visibility of juvenile corrections for a brief time as it brings the agency in contact with new environmental elements or alters slightly its relationship to old ones. Consistent with this explanation, while hardly confirming it, is the positive correlation of .32 between the number of reorganizations and the composite measure of environmental activity. Still another explanation may be that reorganization startles agencies into action by necessitating that they make a good initial impression on their superiors as well as by providing them with something of a "honeymoon" period in which to experiment with ideas previously greeted with indifference. Unfortunately there are no data with which to test these last two points.

Conclusion

Because so little systematic empirical research has been carried out on the impact and dimensionality of task environments, this investigation has of necessity been exploratory in the extreme. In connection with the socioeconomic environment, there was a substantial amount of research and some small amount of theory that could furnish the outlines of a frame of reference from which to comment on the findings—to gauge their consistency and potential generality. This is much less true here.

One of the most interesting implications of the findings is that, unlike the situation thought to prevail in most of the private sector and in some parts of the public sector, consumers, suppliers, and regulators have relatively little *positive* impact on whether or not the bureaucracy innovates—that is, on whether or not deinstitutionalization takes place. By failing to be active or take an interest in the field, environmental elements can prevent substantial deinstitutionalization, but there is little evidence that their demands bring it about.

Part of the reason why there is not a more significant relationship between environmental demands and innovations seems to be that environmental groups rarely possess strong, programmatically specific priorities. They may possess strong correctional ideologies, but they are uncertain about how to operationalize them; nor does greater participation/interest in correctional policy making seem to result in an increased "positive" (demand-centered) impact for the priorities of environmental groups: The correlation between priorities and outcomes is not appreciably greater in those states where environmental groups are very active than in those states where they are disinterested. Despite their potential power in decision making made possible by their integration into a collective decision process, the values of environmental elements do not appear to be defining the "worth" of this innovation, although their "interest" appears to be an important resource for the bureaucracy.

These data are neatly consistent with and help us understand the case study finding that agency executives spend more time in trying to generate interest in the field of corrections than in trying to win groups over to a specific ideological perspective. The latter appears to be unnecessary: One-to-one congruence between their philosophies and those of environmental groups is only marginally relevant to policy implementation. What little data there are indicate that across the states the ability of the bureaucracy to increase the level of participation of environmental groups is slight but it does exist. While generalizations are perhaps risky, the amount of effort expended by public service agencies of all varieties to maintain visibility for their domains suggests that the state of affairs in juvenile corrections is not idiosyncratic. Chapter 6 will contain a more extended discussion of environmental demands and constraints and the implications of the similarity of the functional forms generated by both the principal socioeconomic and task environment determinants.

Many of the implications of the failure to find any significant and stable relationship between commonly utilized political variables and our nonfiscal policy output have already been discussed, but there is one that has not been brought out. This stems from the finding that not only are political variables unrelated to the dependent variable, but they are also unrelated to the priorities of the governor, legislature, and other environmental units, their amount of participation in the field, and their behavior vis-à-vis the corrections agency (e.g., amount and initiation of contact and so on). Thus, in no case was there a substantial correlation between, for example, legislative professionalism or malapportionment and those variables that would be expected to intervene between them and policy outputs. We have been led to believe that a more professionalized legislature will hold more "progressive" views, demand more statistical information from agencies, and force administrators to testify more often in defense of their policies, independent of any assertion that professionalism would have an impact on policy. The absence of these expected relationships introduces a note of skepticism about the entire chain of reasoning that has been proposed and suggests the potential weakness of more than one link.

Finally, the failure of environmental-group heterogeneity and frequency of contact to be correlated with deinstitutionalization draws attention to a rather important issue in the development of a theory of innovation: the relative importance of the search phase versus the implementation phase.[h] For a number of reasons having to do with the kinds

---

[h]Authors have begun to note this distinction as well as to predict that a variety of structural variables (e.g., centralization) are alternatively functional and dysfunctional to innovation depending on whether the organization is in the process of searching for or trying to implement an innovation [see Zaltman et al., 1973; Rogers, 1975]. However, no author has yet attempted to discuss which phase tends to be the most important and under what conditions.

of innovations studied, and the operationalization of the dependent variable, emergent theories of innovation have tended to be heavily search-oriented and have attributed much of the variation in the "innovativeness" of individuals and organizations to the amount of information they receive. It is only a slight overstatement to say that there are those who believe that once the search processes of a unit are explicated, its adoption behavior will be explained.

Yet while there is certainly merit in a search-oriented view of innovation, it seems obvious that there are some situations in which it can lead us astray. Familiarity with the merits of a new drug is undoubtedly a fine predictor of its usage among doctors, whereas familiarity with the characteristics of a new model Rolls-Royce or an innovative abortion law is just as undoubtedly not highly related to their adoption by drivers or states. It is not unusual (especially in the realm of public policy) for virtually all potential adopters of an innovation to be aware of it *before* it is adopted by any of them. Examples range from seat belts to the use of educational vouchers and the negative income tax. In these cases the relevance of sheer quantity of information to adoption may be diminished.

There are reasons to believe that deinstitutionalization falls into this category. There was never any hint that bureaucrats in non-deinstitutionalized states failed to innovate because they lacked information about it. Negative findings such as these argue for a reassessment of the role of information in adoption behavior from a point of view that recognizes the likelihood that its impact is variable.

5

The Impact of Bureaucratic Variables and Executive Characteristics

This chapter focuses on how variations in the characteristics of state juvenile corrections bureaucracies and their chief executives are associated with deinstitutionalization. These might be viewed as constituting the logical last steps in a methodical progression from the broadest decision-making context—that is, the socioeconomic environment—to the narrowest one—that is, the individual decisionmaker. Not surprisingly, as the focus changes so do the research and theoretical traditions that are relevant. The literature of comparative state policy analysis contains much that relates to the impact of socioeconomic dimensions, considerably less that pertains to the task environment, and almost nothing that has to do with the bureaucracy and its leadership. On the other hand, the sociological and economic literatures dealing with innovation which provided no assistance in Chapter 3 and were only slightly more helpful in Chapter 4 are quite relevant here.

Organizational Structure

As we have seen in Chapter 2, the sociological tradition of innovations research, with its Weberian perspective and interest in organizational design, has frequently been preoccupied with the relationship between organizational structure and innovation. The structural dimension that has received probably the greatest attention and is most frequently mentioned in connection with innovation is centralization [Thompson, 1969; Hage and Aiken, 1967 and 1970; Corwin, 1972; Hage and Dewar, 1973]. Centralization is conventionally defined as the extent to which decision-making authority is concentrated at the top of the organizational hierarchy. It is usually thought to act as an obstacle to innovation by discouraging independent behavior and creative thinking on the part of subordinate personnel and by providing those who hold the reins of authority with ample opportunity to maintain the status quo.

However, a number of authors [Wilson, 1966; Sapolsky, 1967; Zaltman et al., 1973] have argued that while centralization may discourage the generation of ideas within the organization and provide insufficient incentives for subordinates to keep abreast of developments outside the organization, a decentralized structure may be dysfunctional to the *implementation* of innovations. The rationale behind this is that centralization provides the organization with the means to overcome internal conflict and fragmentation that can frustrate successful innovation. Thus, Wilson and Zaltman et al. hypothesize that centralization is negatively related to the "initiation" of innovations but positively related to implementation. On this basis they conclude that "the strategy for the organization may be to utilize more-decentralized procedures during the initiation stage and then more-centralized procedures during the implementation stage" [Zaltman et al., 1973:146].

What expectations do these arguments create with respect to the impact of centralization on deinstitutionalization? To begin with, at least part of the traditional argument would seem to have only limited applicability here. Restrictions on the free circulation of ideas and the quality of organizational intelligence brought about by centralization cannot be expected to have a significant effect on the adoption of an innovation well-known to the leadership of every corrections bureaucracy. In addition, the contention that centralization is negatively related to innovation in general because it increases the opportunity of elites to veto a given innovation and thus preserve the status quo rests to at least some degree on the tenuous assumption that program change is more likely to endanger the position and perquisites of elites than of the rank and file. Deinstitutionalization is one example of an innovation where the opposite is more likely to be true, and it is not difficult to imagine others. Generally, the bureaucratic elite has relatively little to lose. The individuals whose status and jobs are placed at risk by this innovation are not those in the upper echelons of the corrections bureaucracy usually stationed in the agency's central office but those lower-ranking employees who work at the institutions and camps.

Perhaps the strongest argument for the existence of an inverse relationship between centralization and innovation is that centralization frequently raises the decision costs involved in making a policy decision. It is not necessary to assume that any program innovation is likely to violate the interests of the organizational elite in order to postulate that (ceteris paribus) the more individuals who must agree to a policy, the less chance it has of being adopted. If centralization results (as it frequently seems to) in the formation of a hierarchy where the consent of supervisors at each level is a necessary prerequisite for adoption, then this alone appears to be a reasonable enough basis upon which to hypothesize a negative relationship between centralization and innovation [Thompson, 1969].

However, there are additional considerations. Although centralization can, by creating increased bureaucratization, raise the "cost" of reaching decisions, under certain conditions it can substantially reduce these costs, as well as those associated with implementation. When the alternative to increased hierarchical decision making is not autonomous decision making by subunits (which is the traditional assumption) but rather a system where the subunits must give their collective assent according to some consensual decision rule before any adoption can take place, then centralization can act to *reduce* decision costs. This is commonly the basis for the argument that centralized and autocratic decision-making or policy-making structures can function more efficiently than decentralized and democratic ones. It is also at the core of the hypothesis that centralization is positively related to implementation. The belief is that the implementation of an innovation is easier when it is not contingent on its voluntary acceptance by subunits but instead can be mandated by a central authority.

The relevance of both the decision cost and the implementation cost arguments to the adoption of deinstitutionalization is somewhat unclear. In this case centralization is probably not a good indicator of the costs involved in the decision to innovate, because extensive deinstitutionalization cannot be carried out autonomously by subunits nor is there any evidence that the movement to deinstitutionalize has ever been initiated far down the corrections hierarchy.[a] Furthermore, centralization appears unlikely to be related to decreased implementation costs, since the implementation of this innovation is not usually contingent to any great extent on its acceptance and understanding by outlying units. Certainly the movement toward deinstitutionalization is not tied to implementation costs in the same sense that statewide installation of a new drug therapy would depend on personnel in various clinics understanding and accepting it. As often as not, deinstitutionalization involves the establishment of new programs and the hiring of new personnel.

All of these considerations lead to the hypothesis that the centralization of the corrections bureaucracy is not strongly related to deinstitutionalization rates. In order to construct an indicator of agency centralization/decentralization the head of the agency was shown a set of seven decisions and asked to reveal which, if any, were exclusively delegated to residential program executives. Although somewhat less exhaustive than the typical Likert Scale questions probing the extent of participation in various decision areas [Hage and Aiken, 1967], there is every reason to believe that this provided an efficient and reliable indicator of centralization that may be less subject to the biases that can attend "perceived participation" [Mohr, 1975]. Scores ranged from 0 to 7, with a mean of 3.5 and a standard deviation of 1.6. The correlation between this measure and the dependent variable is .02, which implies that agency centralization is basically irrelevant to deinstitutionalization. Of course, it is possible that this lack of a relationship is brought about when the

---

[a]Actually, all available evidence suggests the contrary.

increased decision costs that attend centralization are canceled out by decreased implementation costs, but this seems doubtful for the reasons already stated.

At this point one should be careful to avoid the inference that variations in decision and implementation costs are unrelated to variations in state deinstitutionalization rates. The argument has not been that these dimensions have no impact on innovation but rather that in this instance agency centralization is probably a poor indicator of the decision or implementation costs that might be present. Both are strong theoretical constructs that may eventually occupy an important position in any theory of public sector innovation. The problem for the researcher is to identify the source of variability in decision and implementation costs in a particular setting.

With respect to this innovation, we could reasonably contend that implementation costs are less likely to spring from *within* the bureaucracy than from *outside* it, where the community may be unreceptive to community-based programs and where groups in the environment may be indifferent. Similarly, the main source of variation in decision costs may not be the number of decision points within the agency but the number of decision points created by the necessity of securing the approval of groups in the task environment. Thus we have the basis of a broader concept of centralization defined as the extent to which decision making *in toto* is concentrated in the hands of the bureaucratic elite. We might then hypothesize that the greater this concentration of power, the lower the decision costs since widespread consensus among outside elements is not required to reach a decision.

This thinking resulted in the construction of a measure of bureaucratic autonomy, or the extent to which decision-making power is formally concentrated in the bureaucracy, which has already been referred to in other chapters. Once again the agency director was shown a list of decisions, except that this time he was asked to indicate those that could be made entirely within the bureaucracy without the formal approval of the governor, legislature, or others. The set of eight decisions had been compiled on the basis of the case studies and represented those decisions thought to be the most integral to effecting a change in the status quo. The variation in the responses was encouraging. Scores ranged from 0 to 8, with a mean of 4.1 and a standard deviation of 1.7.

The zero-order correlation between this measure of bureaucratic autonomy, or "system centralization," and deinstitutionalization is .24. This correlation, which is in the expected direction and of a magnitude at least worth noting, provides some evidence that the structure of decision making can have some impact on extent of innovation (as well as time of adoption) *if* variations in it are tied to variations in more "fundamental" dimensions such as decision and implementation costs. However, the fact that agency (i.e., "internal") centralization was not related to the dependent variables suggests that this is not inevitably the case and should not be casually assumed.

The *complexity* of an organization's task structure and the extent it employs diverse professional skills has received only slightly less attention than centralization in sociological research on the relationship between organizational structure and innovation.

Wilson (1966) and Lawrence and Lorsch (1967) have suggested that a diversity of tasks means a diversity of perspectives, a variety which, in turn, produces a creative dialectic that results in the development of innovative products and services . . . . an organization with a variety of occupations has a variety of contacts with its environment, which, in turn, means more ideas about what needs to be done and how it can be done [Hage and Dewar, 1973:279].

In spite of the modest empirical support for the hypothesis that complexity is positively related to innovation [Hage and Aiken, 1967; Hage and Dewar, 1973], certain reservations have been voiced that are virtually identical—for obvious reasons—to those raised in connection with centralization.[b] Wilson [1966], Zaltman et al. [1973], and others argue that the diversity in perspectives and expectations inherent in increased complexity leads to conflict over the allocation of scarce resources and a situation in which it is difficult to achieve consensus on a proposed innovation. Complexity, they contend, will result in the generation of more innovative proposals but it tends to make their adoption and implementation more problematic.

As in the case of centralization, it is difficult to develop any clear a priori expectations in the wake of these conflicting arguments. Again, the salience of deinstitutionalization in the corrections field would seem to minimize any impact that complexity might have purely on the basis of its effect on the quantity and quality of organizational intelligence. However, it is conceivable that a high level of complexity could increase the probability that deinstitutionalization would be placed on the agency's agenda since the greater the diversity in perspectives within the agency the more likely there will be one who favors this innovation. Yet even this assumes that between-group differences in perspectives will be significantly greater than within groups, which is an assumption not supported substantially by the case studies. Interviews with representatives of varying professional backgrounds generally revealed as much variation in the

---

[b]Such findings may be methodologically, as well as theoretically, suspect. When complexity is measured by the "number of diverse tasks," any relationship between it and innovation can easily be confounded by the effects of size and resources.

ideologies and orientations of individuals in the same group (e.g., social workers) as across groups (e.g., social workers versus educators or lawyers).

The difficulties involved in achieving consensus when the organization employs different kinds of professionals could result in a negative relationship between complexity and deinstitutionalization, but this involves the further assumptions that complexity invariably leads to divisiveness and, more importantly, that this resultant conflict will have significant policy consequences. Both assumptions appear to be highly conditional—that is, they depend on the nature of innovation being considered and upon certain attributes of the potential adopting organizations. Whether professional divisions will create conflict depends on the extent to which what is beneficial to one group is costly to another. Obviously this is variable across innovations; the decision to innovate is not a zero-sum game with the gains of one group stemming from the losses of another. Furthermore, the magnitude of the impact that complexity will have on policy outputs (including innovation) depends not only on the differences in the benefit-cost equations but also on the extent to which any resultant conflict is translated into increased decision costs. This in turn depends on the representation of different professional groups among the decision-making elite, the degree of agency centralization, and other factors.

The sixteen case studies revealed no clear indication that a policy of deinstitutionalization would consistently disadvantage any one professional group among the central office staff of juvenile corrections agencies. This is not to say they all were equally in favor of it, only that the decision to innovate could be close to being Pareto optimal—that is, it needn't *disadvantage* any group.[c] In addition, the case studies pointed to the fact that in a number of states that had achieved significant deinstitutionalization, the decision to innovate was anything but collegially arrived at. The more hierarchically imposed the innovation, the less professional group competition could be expected to raise the decision costs.

For all of these reasons, agency complexity was not expected to have any great impact—positive or negative—on state deinstitutionalization rates. A simple measure of complexity was constructed on the basis of a crude breakdown of staff by general field of specialization: behavioral and social science, education, public administration or business, and "other" (primarily humanities and law). Difficulties in obtaining information made

---

[c]Outside the central office (and therefore away from the decision-making elite) there was evidence that the situation was different. For instance, educators and security personnel at the institutions would be disadvantaged by extensive deinstitutionalization since community-based facilities do not employ these personnel. However, these groups were not strongly represented in the central office where decisions were made.

a more detailed breakdown impossible, and as it was, only thirty-three states were capable of providing this information. States were given a score from 1 to 4 based on the number of fields that accounted for at least 10 percent of the nonclerical personnel attached to the agency's central office. The correlation between this measure of complexity and the dependent variable is $-.09$. Because of the possible bias caused by a large number of nonrespondents, various other measures of complexity— ranging from the number of formal divisions to the number of services provided by the agency—were also employed. However, these proved to be equally unrelated to the dependent variable.

Centralization and complexity have been discussed at some length because it is felt that even recent treatments continue to hypothesize that each will have a substantial and consistent impact on innovation on the basis of little empirical evidence and less theoretical justification. Therefore, an attempt was made to demonstrate how questionable and conditional relationships between structural characteristics and innovation may be.

For some reason, the traditional Weberian dimensions of structure tend to be treated as fundamental theoretical constructs that ipso facto have a significant and uncomplicated impact on aspects of organizational behavior.[d] An example of this is the conventional (e.g., Hage and Dewar) expectation about the impact of complexity on innovation. When one attempts to specify the process by which complexity is likely to affect the adoptive behavior of an organization, the number of important qualifications and questionable assumptions that come to mind are staggering. The work of those who distinguish between the effects of complexity (and centralization) in the initiation or adoption stage and its effects during the implementation stage appears to be a step in the right direction, but one wonders how fundamental the distinction is between "stages of innovation" and one doubts whether the impact of complexity is really as consistent even within these categories as we are led to believe; nor is it clear how this contingency theory would explain either negative finding described here.

Wealth and "Slack"

In research in both the sociological and economic traditions, the level of organizational resources (wealth, liquidity, etc.) has proven to be one of the principal determinants of innovation. Furthermore, unlike the theoret-

---

[d]Formalization, the third Weberian dimension of organizational structure usually included in innovation research, has been excluded here because its impact is thought to occur exclusively through its restriction of search processes. (See Hage and Dewar [1973] and Thompson [1969].)

ical justifications for some other hypothesized relationships, the logic behind the expectation that resource levels and innovativeness will be positively related is quite persuasive. Innovations, particularly technological ones, are often costly, and wealthy organizations can better afford them. They can also more easily assume the risks involved in adopting an unproven innovation. In addition, wealthier organizations would seem more likely than poorer ones to possess slack in the form of funds and staff time that can lead to a higher quality of organizational search.

However, we have also seen that there is evidence that even the impact of wealth on innovativeness may be conditional. Recall that Mohr [1969] found that resources interact with the motivation to adopt. In addition, the argument has been made that the impact of resources varies with the innovation or the policy output under consideration. Per capita income or revenue level are generally better predictors of expenditures than of certain types of nonfiscal outputs, and it is hard not to believe that wealth is a better predictor of the adoption of computer-operated typewriters than of affirmative action promotion policy. The possibility has also been raised that organizational wealth or slack might be a better predictor of how quickly an organization adopts an innovation than of how extensively it implements it. It is likely that observers of the photocopying industry would be more surprised if the 3M Company *introduced* an innovation before Xerox than they would be if it chose to *commit a greater proportion* of its resources to a particular innovation.

There is no reason to believe that deinstitutionalization—an innovation that essentially represents a redirection of organizational priorities—will be strongly related to the wealth of the corrections agency or its level of fiscal slack. While wealthier agencies might be the first to experiment with community-based programs, it is not clear how an increase in agency wealth would increase the probability that it would close an institution and become 40 percent deinstitutionalized instead of remaining 25 percent deinstitutionalized.[e] Despite modest start-up costs (which can be covered to some extent by federal grants), deinstitutionalization is certainly not a costly innovation, even if we discount the more exorbitant claims that it will radically reduce total corrections expenditures.

Two separate expenditure measures were employed in the analysis. The first—total residential budget—is an indicator of agency wealth since residential program expenditures typically make up more than 90 percent of an agency's budget. This was seen to be a more accurate indicator of

---

[e]The absence of any noticeable correlation between per capita income and deinstitutionalization might ordinarily be taken as support for this view, but we have already seen that per capita income is a very imperfect indicator of agency expenditures.

available resources than total expenditures because in some states the latter includes funds earmarked for other sorts of services (e.g., probation and parole). The second measure—the per offender expenditure for delinquents in institutions—was intended to come closer to capturing the meaning of organizational slack. While hardly free of imperfections (e.g., the differential cost of supplying services across the states), it was felt that this measure would reflect the amount of slack in the system more accurately than a simple aggregate expenditure measure, especially since variations in per offender expenditures are largely the product of services above and beyond those required for basic maintenance—that is, the variations tend to be caused by differential provision of educational, vocational, and psychiatric services as opposed to differing amounts being spent on food, clothing, and security.

The respective correlations between the two measures and the dependent variable are −.16 and −.04, which indicates that there is no simple relationship between agency fiscal resources or slack and the extent of innovation—although, had the dependent variable been measured by the time at which a state first adopted a community-based program, there may well have been a strong positive relationship. It appears that still another basic tenet of innovation theory is in need of some refinement. Just as significantly, these findings, along with that concerning the impact of per capita income, partially justify the intuition of many political scientists that wealth is not invariably the best predictor of policy outputs.

Size

The impact of size on innovativeness has been investigated extensively by both sociologists and economists, although no one has attempted to integrate their somewhat diverse findings. Rogers and Shoemaker [1973] cite 152 empirical studies that bear on the relationship between size and innovativeness, 67 percent of which support the hypothesis that the two are positively related. Economic theorists from Schumpeter [1934] to Galbraith [1956] have concerned themselves with the effect of size of firm on research and development, and these arguments have been extended to apply to innovation as well as invention [Scherer, 1970; Mansfield, 1963]. The reasoning behind expecting a positive relationship between size and innovativeness is virtually identical (with one addition) to that described in connection with wealth. Larger firms—principally because they possess greater resources—are thought to be able to more easily afford innovations and assume the risks involved. To this is added the advantage of economies of scale held by larger firms. These economies result in a reduction in their per unit cost of innovations and permit them (because their volume of production is greater) to show a substantial profit.

The clear overlap between the size and wealth hypotheses and the typically high degree of multicollinearity between the two variables raise a number of questions that are generally avoided. For example, what is the causal connection between size and wealth, and does size have an impact on innovativeness independent of its relationship with wealth? Size is something of a "conglomerate" variable—that is, any effect it might have is conceptually and statistically entangled with a number of different dimensions. Because of this, doubts have been raised about its theoretical value.

Neither community size, farm size, size of health department, nor size of firm should be accepted hastily as an accurate predictor of innovation. Size itself is not related to innovation by logical necessity; it becomes significant only when it implies or indicates the conceptual variables that are important in themselves [Mohr, 1969:121].

This quotation states that the effect of size may be "contingent" in much the same way as the impact of structural characteristics. That is to say, it may depend on the extent to which—in a given sample of organizations—it is related to wealth and perhaps other factors, just as the impact of centralization may be contingent on the degree to which it is related to decision costs (among other things). The conglomerate character of size helps explain why it is not uncommon to find organization theorists positing a negative instead of the usual positive relationship between size and innovation and may also shed light on why 33 percent of the studies cited by Rogers and Shoemaker did not support the latter hypothesis. For example, Hage and Aiken [1967], among others, emphasize the relationship of size to centralization and bureaucratization rather than wealth and thereby postulate that size will be negatively related to innovation.

The impact of size may also be contingent on the type of innovation being considered and the way "innovativeness" is operationalized. If size were highly related to both wealth and bureaucratization, we might anticipate that it would be positively related to the adoption of a very costly innovation (since wealth would probably be an important determinant of the adoption of this type of innovation) but negatively related to the adoption of an unorthodox power-equalization plan (where the level of bureaucratization would likely be a more important determinant than wealth). Of course, in the case of deinstitutionalization neither the level of agency fiscal resources nor the internal decision costs brought about by centralization appear to be significant determinants. However, size might still have a negative impact on innovation apart from what it might have through its suspected close association with bureaucratization. This involves what, for the lack of a better term, might be called the "diseconomies of scale." These diseconomies result when an increase in size is accompanied by a disproportionate rise in factors (primarily decision and implementation costs) that are dysfunctional to innovation. There is some connection between the diseconomies of scale and bureaucratization, but they are not necessarily identical. Other factors may be at work; there may be more than twice as much organizational inertia in an agency that is twice as large as another, or the amount of vested interests in maintaining the status quo may be more than twice as great. Perhaps it is easier, relatively speaking, for a small state to achieve a reasonably high deinstitutionalization rate than for a large one to do so.

The zero-order correlation between the size of the juvenile corrections agency (as measured both by the number of employees and by the number of offenders incarcerated in residential programs) and the dependent variable is $-.08$.[f] Size appears to be unrelated to innovativeness. However, an examination of the scatter plot depicting the relationship between the number of incarcerated offenders and deinstitutionalization revealed the possibility of a threshold effect. Of the 39 states with less than 950 offenders, 15 fall above the mean on deinstitutionalization. Yet only 1 of the 15 with *more* than 950 offenders has a deinstitutionalization rate above the mean. This difference lends some support to the hypothesis that it is more difficult for large agencies to substantially deinstitutionalize than for small agencies to do so. It is also worth noting that agencies with large offender populations are not located in states that are extremely heterogeneous, and the groups in their environments are no more indifferent than the average. Thus, it is doubtful that the threshold effect is spuriously created.

Thus, although its impact is not statistically significant in the usual sense of the term, agency size appears to function as an obstacle to extensive deinstitutionalization.[g] Up to a certain size, agencies have relatively little difficulty in broadly implementing this innovation, whereas beyond that point, it appears that difficulties mount to formidable proportions.

---

[f]Curiously, both correlations were the same.

[g]Its impact is not statistically detectable in conventional terms because it does not affect the overall means of the two strata, only the amount of variation that exists within them. However, restricted variation is nonetheless a type of effect that possesses a very real substantive and theoretical interpretation. The limitations of the statistical techniques currently in use will be taken up in the conclusion.

Staff Characteristics

Although agency complexity was seen to be unrelated to state deinstitutionalization rates, there are other variables based on staff characteristics that have been discovered to be or are often thought to be determinants of organizational innovativeness. While the implementation of this innovation may not consistently and directly conflict with the interests of any one group of professionals in a correctional agency's central office, it is at least conceivable that one group might favor it more than others, which would result in higher deinstitutionalization rates for states whose agencies are dominated by this group. There is also considerable stress in the sociological tradition placed upon the positive impact of an organization's general level of professionalism—apart from the effect of the "mix" of professionals that is tapped by complexity.

For reasons already given, we would anticipate in the case of well-known innovations such as this one that any impact of the degree to which one or another professional group is differentially represented in the agency's central office would be due not to the varying search patterns of the groups but to the fact that they possess slightly different value patterns and thus are motivated by different incentives or would benefit to different extents. However, we have already observed that there were no clear indications that groups in the central office differed significantly in their estimation or support of community-based programs. One explanation for this is that the groups represented are not basically much different in their perspectives. Educators, social workers, and public administrators may tend to hold relatively similar values, especially when their jobs are not being threatened. Still another explanation for which the case studies supplied impressionistic support is that the extent to which a state will deinstitutionalize is primarily a decision made by the director and a small cadre of handpicked advisors.

At any rate, the case studies created the impression that agency domination by a particular professional group—roughly estimated by the percentage of central office staff trained in the different fields—would not prove to be a good predictor of deinstitutionalization. The lefthand side of Table 5–1, which lists the correlations between the percentage of central office staff belonging to each group and the dependent variable, confirms this impression. All the relationships are weak.

Educational or professional level is among the most widely researched characteristic of individual innovators and has frequently, but not invariably, proved to be related to innovativeness [Rogers and Shoemaker, 1973:354]. The amount of research on the impact of the educational level of staff or executives within an organizational context is not nearly as great and the results have been somewhat more ambiguous

Table 5–1
Correlations of Staff Specializations and Degree Level with
Deinstitutionalization

Social science (%)	−.15	L.B.A. (%)	.13
Education (%)	.04	B.A. (%)	−.30
Public administration		Graduate training (%)	−.02
and business (%)	.07	Graduate degree (%)	−.06
Other (law and		J.D. (%)	insufficient variation
humanities) (%)	.14		
		Ph.D. (%)	.42

[Baldridge and Burnham, 1975:168; Mansfield et al., 1971:199]. Again, we would anticipate that should educational level be related to deinstitutionalization, it would be caused by differences in values and incentives rather than by the effect of educational level on organizational search. We might expect that as the percentage of personnel with higher degrees increases, there would be more deinstitutionalization, since the ideology of professionalism looks favorably upon innovativeness. Professional associations tend to confer prestige upon individuals who are innovative or work for an innovative organization. On the other hand, as we have noted the case studies did not reveal that staff input into the decision to deinstitutionalize was great.

The set of correlations listed on the righthand side of Table 5–1 appears to be consistent with the traditional hypothesis that educational level is positively related to innovativeness. There is a tendency for agencies with a high percentage of staff with only B.A.s to have deinstitutionalized less than agencies with fewer such staff. The opposite appears to be true for Ph.D.s. Unfortunately, both correlations are inflated by the existence of an outlier. The juvenile corrections agency in Massachusetts, which has the highest deinstitutionalization rate in the nation, is staffed by less than 5 percent B.A.s and 60 percent Ph.D.s. To appreciate how atypical this last figure is, it is necessary to know that only ten agencies have any staff with Ph.D.s and only one agency has a staff where as many as 20 percent of the personnel hold that degree. When Massachusetts is deleted from the data set, the correlations change to −.26 and −.04, respectively. It now becomes more difficult to interpret this set of findings. There is still some evidence that the percentage of staff with relatively little professional training is negatively related to innovativeness (if we are willing to dismiss the "less than B.A." correlation), but the corollary finding concerning Ph.D.s has evaporated. Various methodological ploys were subsequently attempted (e.g., subtracting the percentage of staff with low educational level from the percentage with a high level of education) in order to remove the ambiguity and permit a straightforward interpretation but all resulted in correlations below .15. These negative findings plus the magnitude of the percent-Ph.D. correlation once the outlier is eliminated seem to indicate that the educational level of staff has little to do with the implementation of our innovation—at least at present. There is really no way to predict on the basis of only this evidence what would occur if other agencies were to employ large numbers of Ph.D.s.

In addition to the above, the average length of staff tenure, the percentage of staff belonging to unions, and the extent of civil service coverage were examined, but none were significantly related to deinstitutionalization. An attempt was also made to see whether any of the staff characteristics mentioned possessed a conditional impact that was tied to agency centralization or autonomy. Although it was "reasonable" to hypothesize that the impact of staff attributes would interact with these variables, the results were also negative in every case.

Together with the negative impact of complexity these findings argue fairly persuasively that characteristics of correctional agency staff have little bearing on whether or not that agency (and the state) will deinstitutionalize. Of course, it is always possible that lack of positive findings can be attributed, at least partly, to the absence of more refined measures. Greater insight (and higher correlations) may have emerged had data been gathered on the particular subfields (e.g., psychology, social work) in which staff had been trained. Or there may have been a payoff in carefully searching out those staff in each agency who form the policy-making elite and in concentrating on that group rather than on all central office personnel. It might also have been wiser to gather attitudinal data directly in addition to examining what were thought to be likely sources of variations in staff perspectives (e.g., educational level).

Such data were not collected, for basically the same reasons that led to the hypotheses that there would be no significant relationship between complexity or the educational background of staff and the dependent variable—that is, because the observations made during the case study phase provided no indications that staff characteristics were particularly important as determinants of deinstitutionalization. Staff data were gathered on the few dimensions reported above because of the emphasis they had received in the literature and because regardless of how methodically case studies are conducted, they can fail to identify the impact of inconspicuous variables such as educational background and years in office. However, as we have just seen, the results obtained on the basis of these data are consistent with initial impressions. Thus, while considerably more detailed information could have been gathered on staff characteristics, there was and is no clear theoretical or empirical justification for doing so.

Performance Gaps

If one agrees, at least provisionally, with the tentative assertion that socioeconomic heterogeneity and environmental activity act principally as resource constraints on the bureaucracy rather than as demands, we have the outlines of a theory of deinstitutionalization that appears to emphasize resources (although not fiscal ones) and constraints over motivations or incentives. Perhaps these findings are indicative of a situation in which the motivation or need to innovate is uniformly great (or at least that the differences among states are negligible), while the constraints on state agencies vary considerably and thus are capable of explaining the variation in the extent to which the innovation has been adopted.[h] If one considers the recidivism rates of juvenile offenders— *which are uniformly high across the states*—to be the principal determinant of "need," this explanation is a forceful one.

Certainly there has been little hard evidence presented up to this point to suggest that other potential sources of need or demand are important. Crime rate, a socioeconomic indicator of need, was found to have no relationship to deinstitutionalization rates; and the priorities of environmental groups, which can be viewed as demands, were only weakly related. Staff characteristics thought to be indicative of various patterns of internal demand also had little or no impact. However, several sources of motivations have not been examined yet. One, which will be looked at in another section, is the ideology of the agency executive; another has to do with the existence of "performance gaps."

A performance gap consists basically of a discrepancy between what the organization is accomplishing and what it could be accomplishing [March and Simon, 1958]. The existence of a performance gap can lead to innovation—which is seen as a way to eliminate this gap—when it is perceived by environmental groups who then put pressure on the organization to change, or when the organization becomes conscious of the gap more or less independently and perceives some benefit to be gained by its elimination. In the field of corrections we would anticipate that the basis for estimating what the corrections agency "could" be accomplishing would tend to be even more subjective than usual. For instance, there is little consensus on the extent to which recidivism or juvenile crime can be reduced, and any dissatisfaction an agency or environmental group may feel toward the rates in their states would not be based on any nationally accepted goal or even recognized norm.

Perhaps the best available indicator of an externally perceived per-

---

[h]It is important to note that this is not at all the same as saying that need is irrelevant to adoption.

formance gap in the area of juvenile corrections is the level of environmental-group dissatisfaction. Three ways such dissatisfaction could be expected to manifest itself are (1) the level of media criticism, (2) the formation of a special legislative committee (within the past three years) to investigate juvenile corrections, and (3) the formation of a similar but gubernatorially inspired investigating committee.[i] Yet it turns out that they are unrelated to deinstitutionalization rates both individually and when aggregated. Although we might have expected the kind of pressure for change that these indicators of dissatisfaction represent, it appears to have no impact on agency innovativeness across the nation as a whole.

Another sort of performance gap that might be expected to affect state deinstitutionalization rates is the difference between the effectiveness or efficiency of institutions versus community-based programs. Since very few states attempt to monitor the relative effectiveness of the two types of programs (in terms of recidivism, educational achievement, or subsequent employment), it is impossible to see whether there is an connection between their differential effectiveness across the state states' deinstitutionalization rates. Of course, the fact ally do not possess such information also means t decisions on it. However, those with at least one gram do possess information on the relative c facilities, and this can be used for policy making be used to quickly calculate the savings that wo were transferred from institutions to group homes was therefore thought that the difference in the per o two types of facilities might be perceived by the bureau groups as an indicator of the degree to which an "effici mance gap existed. The greater the difference between the tw greater the incentive (from the perspective of cutting c to deinstitutionalize.

One might question whether the prospect of potential savings is eally likely to motivate the bureaucracy to innovate, especially in light of the thesis formulated by Downs [1967], Niskanen [1970], and others that emphasizes that agencies attempt to maximize their budgets. Actually the two views are not necessarily in opposition. The experiences of several states have demonstrated that while deinstitutionalization tends to redis-

[i]The formation of special (blue ribbon) committees by the legislature or the governor to investigate the operation of juvenile corrections is a common response to (and subsequent source of still more) dissatisfaction. Other possible indicators of environmental group dissatisfaction and performance gaps, such as executive turnover and budget cuts, were also considered for inclusion but were eventually dismissed because of unreliability. For example, we were aware of too many instances when the agency director left voluntarily or was promoted.

tribute expenditures from one type of program to the other, it does not reduce the total corrections budget. On the contrary, it has occasionally resulted in substantial increases to that budget.[j] Furthermore, legislative and executive staff are likely to have access to such basic cost data, which creates the possibility that such groups could develop an unfavorable impression of the agency's fiscal responsibility if its policies indicated it was insensitive to the apparent opportunity to cut costs. Therefore, to avoid the prospect of future budget cuts (or no budget increases), a large cost differential may push the agency in the direction of deinstitutionalization.

The correlation generated by the per offender cost differential between the two kinds of programming and the dependent variable is .22. The relationship is in the predicted direction, but its magnitude is not impressive. The potential savings of community-based programs would appear to provide an incentive to deinstitutionalize, but only a slight one. Still, it is worth noting if only because it is, aside from the priorities of environmental groups, the only measure of incentives that has been found to have any relationship with innovativeness.

Executive Characteristics

The impact of executive characteristics is one of the few topics in innovations research that has often been empirically dealt with by both economists and sociologists. Age, education, social status, cosmopoliteness, professionalization, activism, and ideology are among those characteristics whose effect is commonly investigated. Overall, the findings have again been quite mixed. Although in the case of each of these variables there is a conventionally accepted hypothesis and theoretical argument, it is disconcertingly easy to find numerous contradictory examples [Downs and Mohr, 1975]. While the existence of these contradictory findings implies that the impact of executive characteristics is contingent on properties of either the organization or the innovation, no one—aside from Mohr [1969]—has postulated a theory that explicitly recognizes this.

All of the evidence gathered in the case studies and much of the structured interview data already presented point to the potential importance of the juvenile corrections agency's chief executive in determining

---

[j]There may be several reasons for this. In a number of cases, withdrawing offenders from institutions did not reduce the total amount spent on institutions; instead it only increased the per-offender cost for institutional care. In other instances the initiation of community-based programs seems to have heralded (and made possible) the development of a variety of new services (e.g., nonresidential and prevention programs) which resulted in an expanded budget.

policy outputs. Even the most casual observer of the field cannot help but notice the extent to which directors come to personify the entire state juvenile justice system to their colleagues, environmental groups, and the public. This is particularly true of executives in states that have acquired reputations for being "innovative." Almost invariably the directors of the agencies in these states have become national figures in their profession and are considered to be largely responsible for their states' accomplishments. It is commonplace for an executive to be credited with "turning the system around" or "rebuilding the system," and objective measures of change (e.g., budget size, number of new programs) frequently indicate that these are more than mere figures of speech. Furthermore, the relative lack of external influence through demands, caused partly by the inability of environmental groups to unilaterally establish detailed priorities, and the general absence of objective evaluative criteria would seem to provide the executive with wide discretion both in setting the agenda for major policy changes and day-to-day administration. Since case study observations also suggested that the director is usually the focus of a centralized policy-making system within the agency, that position can be a powerful one indeed.

It was initially thought that the more years agency directors had worked in the field of juvenile corrections, the less progressive and innovative they were likely to be and the more attached they would be to the status quo. However, the case studies provided no real evidence that this was true, and the correlation between executives' years of experience in the field and deinstitutionalization is only $-.07$. Similar reasoning, plus the belief that newly appointed executives might be expected to do something new led to the hypothesis that the longer executives had been in office, the less likely they would be to press for change, but this hypothesis was not supported by the data ($r = -.04$).

Other executive background characteristics also proved to be only slightly connected with agencies' deinstitutionalization rates. During the conduct of the case studies it was observed that several states had rapidly deinstitutionalized shortly after a director had been hired from outside the state. This led to the hypothesis that outsiders were more likely to innovate than insiders principally because they had not been socialized to current practices and there was no chance that their appointment was a reward for loyalty to the existing system. However, when the fifty states were analyzed, no such relationship was discovered. Furthermore, no relationship emerged between the executive's field of specialization and the dependent variable, although it should be noted that the amount of variation in specialization was not great. Level of education (the majority of executives held master's degrees) was positively related to agency innovativeness, which is consistent with the traditional hypothesis relating the two, but the correlation was only .13.

Because of the lack of variance in the professionalism of agency directors as measured by their fields of specialization and educational level, it was believed desirable to gather somewhat more direct data on their "cosmopoliteness" and "centrality" in the corrections profession. Research in the sociological tradition has generally supported the hypothesis that these attributes are positively related to innovativeness in the individual [Rogers and Shoemaker, 1973], and political scientists like Walker [1969] and Browning [1969] stress their importance as determinants of policy innovation on the organizational and state levels. Yet in this case there was little reason to suspect the professional cosmopoliteness of the director would be an important determinant of innovativeness. Although it is common for professional associations to publicly support some implementation of community-based programs, few have come out solidly behind extensive deinstitutionalization and most contain a conservative contingent of substantial size that remains strongly committed to institutional treatment. Thus, while the attachment of a director to a number of professional associations might provide some incentive to experiment with community-based programs in order to be recognized as being on top of recent developments in the field, it would be unlikely to place any pressure on the director to radically deinstitutionalize or to reward him or her greatly for doing so.

Executives were asked the number of professional associations to which they belonged and the number of professional conferences they had attended in the past year.[k] The respective correlations of the two measures with deinstitutionalization are $-.03$ and $+.04$, which represent an almost perfect lack of association in both cases. The relationship of agency directors to their profession, at least as measured by these two variables, appears to have little to do with how deinstitutionalized their agencies are. It turns out that this nonrelationship is not due to correctional executives' having no impact on agency innovativeness (as will become apparent below) but to the fact that their professional ties are poor indicators of their ideologies and priorities.

Despite their generally similar professional and educational backgrounds, extended interviews with agency directors revealed radically different administrative styles and correctional philosophies. Some administered their agencies in an archetypally reactive fashion, never initiating contact with external groups and rarely asking for more than a nominal budget increase from the governor and legislature in order to keep things quiet. Others were aggressively proactive, by constantly traveling around the state and attempting to build interest in juvenile corrections and forever asking for nonincremental increases in the budget. Some

---

[k]Both are numerous in the field of juvenile corrections. The responses ranged from 1 to 12 for professional associations and from 1 to 20 for conferences.

proved to be militantly in favor of community-based alternatives and against institutions, while others were equally committed to traditional corrections.

Whatever their administrative style or correctional orientation, the vast majority of agency directors are sophisticated professionals who were well aware they were being interviewed by an academically based, federally funded research project. In the course of a lengthy interview invariably containing a considerable amount of casual and off-the-record conversation, the interviewers had no difficulty obtaining a fairly good impression of where the executive stood on issues such as deinstitutionalization and due process, but problems sometimes arose during the "formal" administration of certain questions that sought to probe executive values and priorities. From the experience gained during the exploratory case studies it was known that in juvenile corrections there exist more or less homogenous ideologies cultivated by correctional executives for the public and for "interested others," such as liberal interest groups and academic researchers. In brief, the one presented to the public is based on the desirability of treatment and rehabilitation and the need to improve the current state of the art in these, within the context of recognizing the paramount importance of community protection.[1] When confronted with "interested others" this public philosophy is altered slightly. The necessity of community protection is played down, while the need for innovative treatment alternatives like community-based programs is given special emphasis. This created the danger that the response to value questions would reflect only what the director thought the interviewer wanted to hear, thereby resulting in correspondingly little variance.

Three questions that were developed are believed to have reliably characterized the directors' positions on certain ideological and policy issues. The first asked what importance the directors ascribed to upgrading vocational and treatment programs in the institutions. This was expected to tap their commitment to institutionalization as the primary mode of rehabilitation. A second question asked the directors the extent to which they agreed with the statement "The operation of residential facilities (both institutional and community-based facilities) should be handled by state rather than local or private agencies." This was designed to tap the directors' commitment to the traditional method of administering the provision of correctional services as opposed to more innovative methods associated with community-based facilities (e.g., purchase of

---

[1]A more elaborate version of this basic public philosophy can be found in the annual plans each state must submit to LEAA to be eligible for federal grants. Much of the language in these plans is perfectly interchangeable from one to another, and states have been known to copy each other's planning language word for word.

services).[m] A third question asked the extent of agreement with the statement "The abolishment of closed institutions would represent a real danger to communities throughout the state." This was designed to reveal how necessary the director believed secure institutions to be to the maintenance of community protection.

All three measures were hypothesized to be negatively related to deinstitutionalization. The data supported these hypotheses by generating correlations of $-.31$, $-.40$, and $-.21$, respectively. Because these questions were intended to capture different facets of the directors' correctional orientation that would figure into their overall evaluation of deinstitutionalization, it seemed appropriate to combine them into a single index to measure their cumulative effect.[n] The zero-order correlation between this aggregate index and the dependent variable is $-.46$, which indicates that a cumulative effect does exist and that it is a substantial one. It appears that a significant *motivational* determinant of innovation has finally been uncovered. Furthermore, the fact that none of these four variables is correlated at above .30 with socioeconomic heterogeneity or environmental group activity helps assure us that the relationships are not spurious ones.

The question now arises whether the impact of executive ideology is similar under all conditions or whether it is contingent on other factors, specifically, on the amount of resources available to the agency or its director. As we have already observed, in his study of innovation in public health organizations Mohr [1969] postulated the existence of a multiplicative relationship between public health officer ideology and fiscal resources. However, unlike the innovations Mohr studied, the implementation of deinstitutionalization does not appear to be contingent on agency wealth. And, as expected, agency wealth and executive ideology do not relate to the dependent variable in a multiplicative fashion; the cross-product term created by the two variables turns out to be nonsignificant when included in a multiple regression equation. In the case of deinstitutionalization it seems more reasonable to assume that *agency autonomy* is the salient resource. The more autonomy the agency possesses, the more discretion we would suppose the director to have vis-à-vis the environment, and the less time and energy the director would have to devote to complex negotiation and bargaining.

To test for the existence of interaction between executive ideology

---

[m]Of the offenders in community-based facilities, 83% are in programs operated by local or private agencies, with state participation limited to funding and monitoring.

[n]This single index should not be confused with the sort of dimension discovered through factor analysis. The justification for combining these measures is not the high interrelationship among them—quite the contrary. It is the belief that they have a similar negative impact on the dependent variable which is *cumulative*.

and agency autonomy, the states were divided into two groups: one (N = 18) in which juvenile corrections agencies were highly autonomous, and one (N = 30) in which they possessed relatively low autonomy. If interaction of the type hypothesized exists, we would expect the correlation between deinstitutionalization and ideology to be higher in the first stratum than in the second. The results are striking. In states in which agency autonomy is high, the correlation between executive ideology and the dependent variable is −.81; where autonomy is low, the correlation drops to −.18.[o] From the point of view of regression coefficients, a unit change in director ideology has 4.5 times the impact on deinstitutionalization in the first stratum than in the second. However we look at it, executive ideology is a markedly better predictor of innovation when agency autonomy is high.

Since the above provides a clear indication that interaction does exist between executive ideology and agency autonomy, it is appropriate that we try to specify the nature of the interaction as accurately as possible. One possible test of Mohr's hypothesis that motivation and resources are multiplicatively related to innovation is by the addition of a simple cross-product component to a multiple regression equation that regresses deinstitutionalization rate on ideology and autonomy. Thus,

$$D = \beta I + \beta A + \epsilon$$

becomes

$$D = \beta I + \beta A + \beta (I \cdot A) + \epsilon,$$

where D = deinstitutionalization rate, I = director ideology, A = agency autonomy, and ϵ = the disturbance term. If the second equation can explain a significantly greater portion of the variance in the dependent variable than the first, then we have evidence that a multiplicative relationship exists. The results of adding the cross-product term were initially encouraging. Together, executive ideology and agency autonomy explain 26 percent (multiple R = .51) of the variance in deinstitutionalization rates; with the addition of the cross-product term this increases to 37 percent (multiple R = .61), which is a significant increase. However, an examination of the scatter plot depicting the relationship between the dependent variable and the cross-product term revealed that the increase in variance explained was probably the result of a single outlier. When this case was removed from the data set, the cross-product term failed to result in a significant increase in explained variance over the two-variable

---

[o]Similar differences between correlations in the two strata were obtained for each of the individual variables from which the cumulative index is constructed.

model. We are forced to tentatively conclude that executive ideology and agency autonomy do not relate to deinstitutionalization in a simple multiplicative fashion. Various other functions (principally exponential ones) relating the two explanatory variables were experimented with, without success.

The above analysis suggests that the interaction between ideology and autonomy, which was revealed by the subgroup correlations of $-.81$ and $-.18$, consists of a sharp threshold effect. This means that executive ideology does not have a steadily increasing impact with increases in agency autonomy; rather, it has a fairly consistent impact on innovation at various levels of agency autonomy until a certain threshold is reached, at which point that impact alters dramatically. We can further estimate that this threshold point is located approximately at the level of autonomy where we decided to divide the states into two strata.

A possible explanation for this threshold effect might be the differential importance of the decisions out of which the index of agency autonomy was constructed. The findings reveal that there is not an equal probability that an agency that makes two of the eight decisions autonomously will make *any two* decisions. Several of the decisions that may be particularly important in the implementation of deinstitutionalization, notably "opening a new residential facility" and "closing a residential facility," were rarely made by agencies in the low-autonomy stratum but are commonly the prerogative of agencies in the high-autonomy stratum. If we hypothesize that the ability to unilaterally make one or both of these decisions dramatically increases agency autonomy, and the power of the director, then we can understand why the analysis would reveal a threshold.

Imitation as a Determinant of Innovativeness

We have seen how Gray [1973], Collier and Messick [1973], and particularly Walker [1969] have stressed the importance of specifying communication and reference patterns in order to understand variation in the adoption of policy innovations by states and nations. Begging the question for the moment of whether such an interactionist or imitation-oriented explanation is in fact independent of one that emphasizes prerequisites or determinants, can we find any evidence to support the hypothesis that we can better predict state deinstitutionalization if we know something about those states agency directors are monitoring?

To avoid having to infer the importance of imitation and search processes indirectly from innovation scores (which has been the method used in the past), the agency directors were asked to name those states that they (a) thought had the best juvenile justice systems, (b) looked to for new ideas, and (c) believed to be the most similar to their own. Even on a descriptive level the replies to these questions provided insight into the communication and reference-group patterns that exist in juvenile corrections. Perhaps most striking is the fact that these patterns are not strongly based on contiguousness or region. Not only did directors frequently name states outside their region as having the best juvenile justice systems, but the majority named more states outside than inside their regions as sources of new ideas. Approximately 40 percent of the directors even went outside their region in choosing states most similar to their own in terms of the problems they faced as well as their policies.

To test the hypothesis that the search and reference patterns of the director are determinants of agency policy outputs, each agency was assigned a score based on the average deinstitutionalization rate of the states to which the director looked for new ideas. If the reference-group hypothesis were correct, we would expect a close correspondence between the agency's deinstitutionalization rate and those of the reference states. Yet we discover extremely wide variation in the deinstitutionalization rates of the states named by individual directors and a correlation of only .22 between the two rates.[p] This indicates that some imitation may be taking place but that it is not a principal determinant of this particular policy innovation. Fortunately, the modest size of this relationship spares us the necessity of engaging in the complicated task of trying to figure out whether states are copying each other or merely reinforcing decisions made on the basis of purely internal factors by monitoring agencies with similar resources and inclinations.

Once again one must be careful not to overgeneralize from this finding. Had we been attempting to explain the variation across states in the time at which they first installed a community-based program, imitative behavior may well have been readily apparent. It is probably wiser to settle for an interim hypothesis to the effect that imitation is a better predictor of time of adoption than of depth of adoption—where various internal incentives and constraints are much more likely to become important.

Conclusion

From a substantive point of view, this exploration of the impact of bureaucratic and executive characteristics has increased our ability to

---

[p]For those who believe that while directors might utilize one reference group during the search process and another for the decision to adopt, the correlation between agency deinstitutionalization rate and that of the states believed to be the "most similar" is .23.

explain variation in state deinstitutionalization rates—strikingly so in that subset of states in which juvenile corrections agencies are granted considerable decision-making discretion. Despite the contentions of many researchers that within an organizational context the values and orientations of individuals (including the elite) are far outweighed in importance by structural factors and have a marginal impact at best [Hage and Aiken, 1970; Baldridge and Burnham, 1975], the ideology of the director was seen to be easily the most powerful determinant of those examined, although its impact is tied to agency autonomy. Both the case study and interview data attest to the basic validity of the Nelson and Winter argument that it is common for nonmarket firms to possess a good deal of discretion (although the extent of that discretion obviously varies) and that this necessitates a careful analysis of the values of those directing such organizations. In the field of juvenile corrections the values of the organization appear to be synonomous with those of the agency director. A point of interest in connection with the impact of director ideology that has not been stressed is that director ideology shows little evidence of being "role-determined." Complexity, centralization, staff professionalism, and wealth, are all poor predictors of executive orientation.

Other variables, such as decision-making autonomy, the differential costs of institutional and community-based placements, and the average deinstitutionalization rate of the director's reference group, appear to have a slight but observable impact on the degree of agency innovativeness. In addition, there is evidence that agencies above a certain size are unlikely to deinstitutionalize, in spite of the fact that the overall correlation between size and the dependent variable is only $-.08$.

Equally interesting, from a substantive and prescriptive standpoint, are the negative findings (i.e., the absence of certain relationships). Neither centralization, complexity, nor staff professionalism—dimensions that make up the core of the sociological tradition's organizational design prescriptions for "ensuring" that an organization will be innovative—are related to deinstitutionalization rates. Wealth and organizational slack also proved to have no impact (additive or interactive) on the adoption of this innovation. These negative findings would be startling and perhaps even suspect if they were not so eminently plausible given what is known about this particular innovation and the agencies that are its potential adopters. Of course, it is notoriously easy to come up with post facto, ad hoc hypotheses to justify any findings; but in the case of each of these variables, we saw that a theoretical basis for *expecting* a null finding was implicit in the often confused and complex rationale for linking it to innovativeness in the first place.

From a theoretical point of view, what is particularly significant is that in each instance the argument behind the commonly accepted hypothesis regarding the variable's relationship to organizational innovativeness was shown to depend on certain assumptions about factors (e.g., the cost of the innovation, the importance of information) that can change considerably from one innovation to the next. It also became clear that other assumptions about the manner in which structural and resource variables affect innovativeness are quite tenuous and that their validity varies from one choice setting to another. Such assumptions include the equating of these variables with other, more fundamental and abstract dimensional constructs such as decision costs and conflict. It becomes obvious, when we pause to think about it, that an increase in centralization will not inevitably lead to an increase in decision costs, nor will increased complexity or decreased slack always create conflict. These would seem to be some of the theoretical implications both of the findings presented in this chapter and of the substantial amount of contradictory evidence present in the innovation literature that has tended to go unnoticed [Downs and Mohr, 1975]. However, a full discussion of such matters is the province of the next and final chapter.

6

Summary and General Conclusions

Substantive Findings and Prescriptive Implications

In our examination of the numerous explanatory variables based on characteristics of the socioeconomic and task environments, the correctional bureaucracy, and the agency director, only a handful appeared to be closely linked (either additively or interactively) to variations in state deinstitutionalization rates. To begin with, the evidence suggests that the only dimension of the state socioeconomic environment that is a significant determinant of this innovation is something we have labeled socioeconomic heterogeneity. This dimension is composed of various indicators of social and economic "cleavages" in a state: percent black, income inequality as measured by GINI, and the percentages of the population that are poor and uneducated. It is closely related to (and possibly a major determinant of) the liberality of a state as measured by the percent Democratic vote in the 1968 and 1972 presidential elections and to the political culture of the state in general. The negative correlations between indicators of this dimension and the dependent variable were consistent with the hypothesis that where class and racial differences are deep, there tends to be less community tolerance of—and a more punitive approach toward—deviance, at least partly (it was reasoned) because there is a high probability that the deviants will belong to a stratum of the population that is not fully accepted by the majority and that tends to be excluded from the decision-making process. Conversely, the more *homogeneous* a state's population is with respect to social class, income, and race, the more likely an environment will exist that is conducive to the integration and treatment of delinquents within the community.

Of particular interest was the functional form of the relationship between the indicators of socioeconomic heterogeneity and deinstitutionalization as revealed by an examination of their scatter plots. These turned out to be markedly heteroscedastic in a manner that might be associated with a necessary but not sufficient condition—that is, as heterogeneity increases, the maximum deinstitutionalization rate achieved by any state decreases linearly, but at *all* levels of heterogeneity, there are states with low deinstitutionalization rates. In other words, a knowledge of state socioeconomic heterogeneity aids us in predicting the *maximum* level of deinstitutionalization that a state might achieve but not the *minimum*. Because the functional form of a necessary but not sufficient condition is characteristic of a "resource" constraint rather than a "demand" constraint, we were able to speculate that the liberal and tolerant political culture and climate of public opinion that accompany socioeconomic homogeneity are resources that permit the bureaucracy to innovate *if it desires* but do not *force* it to do so. Thus, the socioeconomic environment appears capable of restricting innovation by withholding necessary resources (specifically, community acceptance of community-based programs) but is incapable of guaranteeing it will take place by creating a high level of demand.

Curiously, the dimension of the correctional agency's task environment found to be the most closely associated with deinstitutionalization rate also related to it in the manner of a necessary but not sufficient condition, or resource constraint. A high level of activity or interest by environmental groups (e.g., courts, legislature, interest groups) in the field of juvenile corrections appears to be another necessary prerequisite for a state to achieve substantial deinstitutionalization, but such interest alone is not sufficient to bring it about. On the other hand, the priorities of environmental elements, individually and collectively, were seen to be only marginal determinants of innovativeness and were thus revealed to be neither necessary nor sufficient prerequisites. Both findings were consistent with observations made during the case study phase of the research that indicated that environmental elements rarely held strong program-specific priorities and that agency directors were commonly much more concerned about the indifference of such groups than with their opposition. We later saw that there were indications that efforts by the agency could successfully increase the amount of environmental-group interest, at least slightly.

The only other characteristic of the task environment that appeared to be a significant determinant of deinstitutionalization was environmental instability as measured by the number of large-scale reorganizations of the state bureaucracy that had taken place in the past five years. Because of the marginal impact of the priorities of environmental agencies and actors, it was argued that the prevalence of reorganizations did not act to bring about innovation by creating an environment characterized by shifting demand patterns, although this is how environmental instability is conventionally hypothesized to cause innovation. Instead the impact was thought to stem from their temporarily increasing the visibility of juvenile corrections and by providing the agency with an incentive to show itself to be innovative.

Attributes of the correctional agency and its personnel that were revealed to have a small but noticeable impact on innovativeness included the decision-making autonomy of the agency, the differential cost of institutional and community-based placement, and the average deinstitutionalization rate of the director's reference group of states. Although size is uncorrelated with the dependent variable, a study of the scatter plot of their relationship revealed that agencies above a certain size were less likely to deinstitutionalize to a significant extent than smaller ones. However, the principal determinant of deinstitutionalization within the bureaucracy was the ideology and priorities of the director—at least when the agency had been granted considerable decision-making discretion.

Case studies revealed directors to be extremely powerful forces within correctional agencies; they were frequently capable of molding the agencies to suit their administrative styles and of effectively determining agency goals and priorities. To this extent juvenile correctional agencies resemble organizations as described in Selznick's *Leadership in Administration* [1957] more closely than they do the modern, archetypal, bureaucracy in which everyone, including the chief executive, can be replaced without significant consequences. Therefore it came as no surprise when data analysis suggested that when the agency is relatively free to determine correctional policy, the values of the director become an excellent predictor of the direction this policy takes.

Even this simplified narrative description of the findings yields important prescriptive implications for proponents of deinstitutionalization, especially when it is combined with the numerous negative findings. One clear lesson to be learned from these findings is the importance of keeping the topic of juvenile corrections on the agendas of environmental groups, thus maintaining its political "visibility." There is evidence that the agency itself can help create such visibility, and doubtless an active interest group organized or controlled by advocates of deinstitutionalization could also do so.

What both should keep in mind is that it appears to be considerably more important to generate and maintain a high level of interest in the area of juvenile corrections than it is to win the legislature, governor, and others over to a specific ideological position that embraces a strong commitment to community-based treatment. Since in this field ideological positions tend to be only vaguely related to specific programmatic priorities, the latter activity would be an inefficient use of time and resources. The proper strategy for proponents of this innovation would seem to be to keep juvenile corrections in the public eye in as nonpartisan and nonideological a way as possible. Of course, proponents must also recognize that while the generation of environmental interest will remove an obstacle to substantial deinstitutionalization, it will provide virtually no insurance that it will take place.

A more indirect tactic that could be used to foster innovation is to encourage the relocation of the juvenile corrections agency within the state bureaucracy. This should be done not because the agency will function more effectively if it is—or is not—placed in a large umbrella agency or consolidated with adult corrections but because such a relocation helps to create visibility and may increase the internal activity of the agency. Actually, a correlation of .32 between the number of reorganizations that have taken place and the extent of deinstitutionalization is hardly justification for actively working for the massive reorganization of the state bureaucracy. Nevertheless, given the opportunity, advocates of this innovation might be wise to support a relocation attempt periodically.

From the standpoint of structural changes, the optimal course of action would be to work to provide the correctional agency considerable decision-making discretion, and perhaps the most appropriate time for instituting the sort of procedural changes this requires is during an administrative reorganization of the type just described. Yet, by itself this tactic, like that of generating environmental interest, cannot be expected to result in a dramatic increase in the deinstitutionalization rate. Increasing the autonomy of the agency will bring about the desired results only if the director possesses a correctional orientation conducive to implementing the innovation. Thus it is necessary for proponents of deinstitutionalization to push for both a correctional agency that is powerful in relation to its environment *and* a director who favors the innovation and will work hard to keep juvenile corrections on the policy agenda of environmental groups.

These prescriptions are quite different from those we might have generated simply on the basis of past research on the determinants of innovation. Such prescriptions would have almost certainly called for a more decentralized correctional bureaucracy, greater staff professionalization, and the devotion of more state funds to the field. Yet, examination of the data provides no reason to believe that any of these tactics would produce the desired results. This does not mean that such tactics are invariably wrong, but it does imply that their utility is not universally high and, furthermore, that the prescriptions commonly offered—like the hypothesized impact of a variety of socioeconomic, task-environmental, and organizational dimensions—are insufficiently sensitive to interaction among characteristics of the choice situation.

Having described the findings in a general way, we can now attempt to summarize them mathematically. The hope here is that we will be able both to estimate with some precision how close we have come to answering the question of why states have deinstitutionalized their juvenile justice systems to widely varying extents and to assign priorities to the various prescriptions based on the impact the manipulation of any one factor is likely to have. Under the best of circumstances the latter goal is not easy to achieve, since it is predicated on a correct partitioning of the variance explained, and this effort can be frustrated by countless problems involving causal ordering, specification and measurement error, and multicollinearity. Unfortunately, in this case conventionally employed statistical techniques are inadequate both to the task of fully summarizing what is known about the determinants of deinstitutionalization and to that of partitioning the variance in order to evaluate the impact of specific variables.

The normal procedure for summarizing the collective impact of explanatory variables is to insert them into a multiple regression equation and then report the percentage of variance explained or the R^2. In this instance we find that socioeconomic heterogeneity, environmental-group activity, agency decision-making autonomy, and executive ideology can together explain 50 percent of the variance (multiple $R = .70$) in state deinstitutionalization rates.[a] This figure is slightly above average for most studies of policy determinants and quite high for one in which the dependent variable is a nonfiscal output and the explanatory variables do not include the usual array of socioeconomic dimensions (per capita income, urbanization, etc.). However, it is misleading for several reasons.

First, the existence of a type of threshold interaction between agency autonomy and executive ideology suggests that the coefficients of these variables and the overall R^2 represent no more than a crude averaging that obscures what is really going on in the data. When we stratify on the basis of autonomy and recalculate the regressions, we find that the same variables are capable of explaining 80 percent (multiple $R = .89$) of the variance when the decision-making autonomy of the agency is high but only 29 percent (multiple $R = .54$) when it is low. Thus the combined explanatory power of the variables is vastly different depending on the extent of agency autonomy, and the R^2 obtained from the single regression equation simultaneously over- and underestimates our ability to explain state deinstitutionalization rates.

Secondly, while the first problem is not totally uncommon and can be dealt with by presenting both R^2s, this statistic is incapable of accurately describing the impact of a necessary but not sufficient determinant. In order for the R^2 to be interpreted as a consistent measure of the degree to which knowledge of the explanatory variable(s) permits us to correctly predict the scores on the dependent variable, there must be nearly homoscedastic variance around the regression line (or n-dimensional hyperplane). When severe heteroscedasticity is present, the accuracy

---

[a]The addition of other variables (e.g., number of reorganizations) does not significantly increase this figure. Using standardized regression coefficients, the resultant equation is $D = -.24$ (heterogeneity) $+ .41$ (environmental-group activity) $+ .23$ (autonomy) $- .34$ (ideology).

with which we can predict a state's score on the dependent variable depends on the *score* of the explanatory variable(s). For example, as the level of environmental-group activity increases, its power as a predictor of the dependent variable decreases proportionately. In the case of both it and socioeconomic heterogeneity the percentage of variance explained changes according to a linear function of their scores. This means that the R^2 from a multiple regression equation containing these variables is a highly unstable average estimate, and its utility as a summary statistic diminishes accordingly.

Finally, R^2 does not include the impact of a variable such as size that appears to affect the dependent variable by restricting its variance above a certain threshold rather than significantly increasing its mean. Because it is uncorrelated with the dependent variable, it technically has no effect; its inclusion does not increase the percentage of variance explained. Yet nonetheless this sort of nonrandom heteroscedasticity is characteristic of a type of impact that possesses a substantive and theoretical interpretation.

In a similar fashion, the existence of interaction and theoretically tractable heteroscedasticity make it virtually impossible to estimate the relative impact of *individual* variables by using any statistic based on or generated by multiple regression. Director ideology has no single impact; it has at least two that are considerably different. Worse yet, the relative impacts of socioeconomic heterogeneity and environmental-element activity continually change depending on where states fall on these dimensions. Furthermore, no commonly employed coefficient can begin to convey what seems apparent from an examination of the scatter plots: These variables function as necessary but not sufficient determinants capable of accurately predicting the maximum but not the minimum amount of deinstitutionalization that will take place. And, of course, according to any sum-of-squares-based statistic, size has no impact at all; even though while not affecting the prediction itself, it does conspicuously affect the accuracy of prediction. Obviously these factors make it difficult to make coherent generalizations about priorities among prescriptions.

The inability of multiple regression or any causal modeling technique based on it either to summarize precisely the cumulative impact of these four variables in a meaningful fashion or to convey fully the manner in which each relates to the policy output is significant. The fact that interaction and interpretable nonrandom heterogeneity not only occur in this data set but totally dominate the findings would seem to indicate that different sorts of statistical techniques must be used to more accurately portray the relationship between policy determinants and outputs.

Implications for Policy Theory

In spite of our inability to statistically characterize the findings fully and precisely, there is no question that the inclusion of attributes of the bureaucracy and its environment has led to our being better able to explain variation in this particular policy output. Falcone and Whittington concluded their research on the political black box by observing that the proverbial Alpha Centaurian could explain policy outputs in Canada as well with data on a few socioeconomic dimensions as he could with all the information on the Canadian political process and institutions they had been able to quantify [1972:50]. This conclusion, which is in keeping with most research on the determinants of policy outputs in the American states, does not apply here. Ignoring for the moment the inadequacies of R^2 as a summary statistic and continuing the metaphor: If the Alpha Centaurian were provided with basic socioeconomic data on per capita income, urbanization, industrialization, and population density, he could explain less than 5 percent of the variance in deinstitutionalization rates.[b] If he were given data on indicators of socioeconomic heterogeneity as well, this figure would rise to almost 25 percent, which is still considerably below the 50 percent figure attained with the inclusion of the task-environmental and the two additional bureaucratic variables (using an additive model).

The inability of most socioeconomic variables to account for substantial variation is consistent with the belief of early critics of the "new orthodoxy" that the impact of the socioeconomic environment diminishes as one moves away from defining policy outputs purely in terms of expenditures or items logically tied to expenditures. However, their corollary belief that under such circumstances political variables would assume substantial importance received no support whatsoever. Malapportionment, legislative professionalism, and other characteristics of the political process had no significant independent impact on deinstitutionalization rates nor did they prove to be the mechanisms through which environmental heterogeneity affects the output. This study must join the multitude of others that have failed to reveal a theoretically or statistically viable relationship between these aspects of state political systems and policy outputs.

Taken together these results do not support the critics of determinants research as much as they do those scholars who, like Lowi and Rourke, have long argued that the governmental bureaucracy possesses a

---

[b]It is interesting to recall that using only three of these four variables, Fabricant was able to account for 72 percent of the interstate variance in total expenditures in 1942.

substantial and independent role in policy making. The implication of their argument, partially borne out by this research, is that it is toward the bureaucracy that analysts must look if they desire to understand the nature of public policy.

This sort of global generalization is useful if only because the bureaucracy has been ignored by comparative policy researchers in favor of characteristics of the legislature and mass politics. However, we must be careful not to casually overestimate the extent to which the bureaucracy shapes outputs *independently* of external demands and constraints. Considering the bureaucracy to be a closed system would undoubtedly be as mistaken as attempting to understand the behavior of a firm or legislature without reference to consumers or interest groups. Almost certainly the decomposability of the bureaucracy from the larger socioeconomic system and the extent of its independent impact on policy is variable, and it is the task of policy theory to make the determinants of that variation explicit. It is difficult to make much headway in this task on the basis of a single study, but by reflecting on the determinants of this innovation, its distinguishing characteristics, and the results of other studies, a number of tentative observations are possible.

To begin with, perhaps the most likely determinant of system decomposability with respect to a given output is the degree to which needed programmatic resources are closely tied to variations in the socioeconomic environment. Traditionally the primary resource has been money; funds for state aid to education, welfare benefits, public housing, and other services. It therefore comes as no surprise that governmental expenditures are often closely related to economic development: Levels of expenditures are tied to budget constraints, which are tied to revenue constraints, which are tied to per capita income and industrialization.

Of course, one should not infer that the links in this chain are invariably or uniformly stable or strong.[c] Categories of expenditures can be traded off in order to stay within budget constraints, revenue constraints can be circumvented (at least temporarily), and differing levels and modes of taxation produce variations in revenue in states with roughly comparable income and industrialization. When we focus on only one expenditure category or one agency, these links can potentially be entirely obscured, although many studies have demonstrated that they still exist—possibly because of the remarkable stability of budget shares over time. Obviously many factors are in operation here that are only imperfectly understood. Is there a tendency for larger categories of expenditures (e.g., welfare, education) to be more closely tied to revenue levels and economic de-

---

[c]For an insightful discussion of how weak the links in the chain can be—particularly between socioeconomic characteristics and revenue constraints—see Larkey [1975].

velopment than smaller ones (e.g., juvenile corrections, parks and recreation)? What, if any, impact does the manner in which the state budget is structured have on the stability of expenditure categories in relation to socioeconomic conditions? Do states tend to trade off expenditures from one substantive area to another using similar decision rules with similar priorities attached to the expenditure categories? These are the sorts of questions that must be answered if we are ever to really understand the link between economic development and expenditure-based outputs.

Had the output under consideration in this study been educational or welfare expenditures and had we focused on either state boards of education or welfare bureaucracies, the impact of per capita income and industrialization would doubtless have been greater and the independent impact of bureaucratic and task-environmental variables correspondingly reduced. In these cases the probability would be higher that such socioeconomic characteristics would act to place a ceiling on agency discretion by limiting the amount of money that could potentially be directed to such ends. In deinstitutionalization we have a policy output in the form of an innovation that costs relatively little, so that there was no reason to expect budget and revenue constraints or state income to be closely associated with the extent of its implementation.[d] On the other hand, the development of community-based corrections does require a certain amount of tolerance and receptivity on the part of the citizenry in order to successfully treat delinquents within the community. Thus a favorable climate of public opinion as indicated by political culture emerged as a resource that has to be present if substantial deinstitutionalization is to take place. Further analysis revealed state political culture to be strongly related to socioeconomic heterogeneity.

The discovery of a dimension of the socioeconomic environment that is unrelated to measures of economic development but is nonetheless a determinant of policy output variation indicates that that environment is multidimensional rather than unidimensional and that its impact on policy does not stem exclusively from the relationship between economic development and the availability of fiscal resources. Further research and secondary analysis of past studies should be carried out to investigate the number of other socioeconomic dimensions that determine the availability of various kinds of necessary resources to the bureaucracy, thereby limiting its ability to independently determine policy outputs.

---

[d]Naturally it would be a mistake to ignore the *indirect* effects of socioeconomic variables. Under some conditions it might be possible for per capita income to be a major determinant of a policy innovation that involved only a minor expenditure because it made possible the hiring of expensive professionals who in turn pushed for the innovation. In the case of deinstitutionalization, however, there was reason to believe (see Chapter 5) that such indirect effects were not present.

The independent impact of the bureaucracy can also be constrained by the absence of necessary resources in its task environment as well as in the socioeconomic one. In the case of deinstitutionalization this task-environmental resource was the interest and activity of environmental groups, which provided visibility to a human service area marginal in terms of the proportion of the state budget devoted to it and the population it serves. Because some formal action by either the legislature, governor, or the judiciary (and not infrequently, all three) is needed to deinstitutionalize to any significant extent, it is necessary that juvenile corrections be on the working agendas of these groups. The findings show that in states where environmental elements are indifferent to juvenile corrections issues, deinstitutionalization does not take place regardless of what the bureaucracy might desire. As the interest and activity of groups in the area increases, the potential for significant deinstitutionalization (but not necessarily its achievement) increases proportionately. This is precisely the opposite of what occurs as the level of socioeconomic heterogeneity increases. It appears that the bureaucracy can manipulate this characteristic of its task environment to some extent just as firms can stimulate interest in their products among their consumers, but there is no evidence that environmental interest can be generated entirely by efforts of the agency.

No other studies have attempted to measure environmental-group activity or issue-area visibility, so there is no way to substantiate the finding that these factors relate to outputs as necessary but not sufficient determinants. However, the emphasis that organization theorists have placed on attention rules, time constraints, and sequential attention to goals [Cyert and March, 1963] supports the view that issue visibility may be an important "resource" determinant when decision making involves a number of elements or groups. Of course, some policy areas and issues are considerably less marginal than others and enjoy a high level of visibility continuously and in all the states. State aid to education, for instance, may inevitably be one of the most important items on the agenda of all groups concerned. Under such circumstances visibility will no longer define the parameters of bureaucratic decision making, and we will have to look elsewhere for the determinants of output variation.

At the present time little is known about the relative importance of dimensions of task environments such as size and complexity, or how those dimensions motivate and constrain the behavior of decisional structures such as public agencies. Research needs to be conducted to identify resources aside from visibility that are lodged in the task environment and to reveal how closely these dimensions are related to the socioeconomic environment and decisional structures.

To this point, the discussion has been confined to ways in which the socioeconomic and task environments limit the discretion of bureaucracies by establishing policy parameters through the control of necessary *resources*. The scatter plots depicting the relationship of both socioeconomic heterogeneity and environmental-element activity to deinstitutionalization were seen to resemble those of resource constraints. Each dimension was strongly related to the upper bound of the plot but unrelated to the lower, restricting the maximum level of deinstitutionalization a state could achieve but not the minimum. This emphasis on resource constraints raises the question of whether and under what conditions policy parameters and hence the independent impact of the bureaucracy or another decisional structure are limited by external *demands* as well as resources. Is it equally common for a certain level of demand to guarantee that a minimum output threshold will be achieved regardless of the structure of the bureaucracy and the values of its officers? Examples where this seems likely to occur quickly come to mind. Expenditures for flood control and unemployment are undoubtedly related to the need for them, and it seems inconceivable that a state with a chronic flood problem or high unemployment would spend nothing. Nevertheless, the findings of this study raise the interesting possibility that in general the relationship between outputs and resources is much more inelastic than that between outputs and demand and that the bureaucracy is correspondingly more responsive to changes in the former than the latter. This can be seen as a further extension of the results obtained by both determinants researchers and process modelers that indicate public expenditures are more a function of wealth and revenues than of demand or need.

However, it is probable that there is no single coefficient of elasticity between demands and policy outputs but that it is variable. A factor that might cause that coefficient to vary is the degree of uncertainty surrounding the efficacy of a given policy. One explanation for why crime rates and therefore the need/demand to reduce crime are unrelated to deinstitutionalization is that environmental groups are highly uncertain about whether such a policy will actually reduce those rates. The priorities of environmental elements with regard to specific program options like the development of community-based programs are vague at least partly because the consequences of the different options are so unclear. Were these consequences less obscure, we might have found a stronger association between environmental priorities (demands) and the dependent variable.

Because a high degree of obscurity and uncertainty surrounds the consequences of many public policies, particularly (but certainly not exclusively) in the area of human services, it should come as no surprise if the relationship between environmental demand in the form of apparent need or environmental-group priorities and policy outputs such as deinstitutionalization is not great. Furthermore, these findings are consistent with the observations of political scientists that have emphasized how the complexity of contemporary problems and the uncertainties surrounding policy alternatives lead elected officials to either delegate policy-making responsibility to bureaucracies or, minimally, permit administrative agencies to structure their agendas and define their alternatives.[e] The central role that uncertainty plays in these arguments suggests the provisional hypothesis that the ability of the bureaucracy to independently determine policy (i.e., its decomposability from its environment) is not constant but is contingent on the degree of uncertainty that surrounds a policy area. The greater the uncertainty the more attenuated will be the relationship between objective indicators of need and output levels.

To this point we have discussed factors that seem likely to affect the decomposability of the bureaucracy's impact on policy outputs, particularly the amount and type of resources connected with an output, the political visibility of a policy area, and the degree of uncertainty surrounding the consequences of policy options. Because these factors can be expected to vary from case to case, it is necessary to refrain from making unconditional generalizations about "the" degree of independent impact the bureaucracy has on public policy. Similarly, even when the circumstances are conducive to the bureaucracy's having a significant independent impact on outputs, the effect of specific characteristics of the bureaucracy may depend on still other factors, which thus makes generalizations about such characteristics even more problematic than about the bureaucracy as a whole.

For example, in the last chapter we saw that variations in agency search procedures were unable to account for any significant proportion of the variation in innovation rates. Two possible explanations for this finding, which appear to conflict with those of Walker, were offered. First, unlike highly technical or unpublicized innovations that may be unknown or not understood by the majority of potential adopters during the early stages of their diffusion, the concept of deinstitutionalization was common knowledge to every correctional agency director long before the first state instituted the innovation on a large scale. In this case large, cosmopolitan, and highly professionalized agencies possessed no informational advantages over small, insulated, and less professionalized ones. Second, the fact that the innovation was measured by the extent of

---

[e]Thus the bureaucracy has a significant "uncertainty absorption" function [Cyert and March, 1963:119] in the political system.

adoption rather than the time of adoption seemed likely to have the effect of reducing the explanatory power of characteristics related to initial or trial adoption (e.g., search-process variables) in favor of characteristics more central to the process of implementation. The discrepancy between these findings and those of Walker, together with the strength of these tentative explanations, suggests that the search process has a variable impact on the adoptive behavior of an organization that depends on the extent to which knowledge about the innovation has diffused prior to adoption, how innovativeness is measured, or both.

It is highly probable that the impact of other organizational variables is also conditional. The negligible effect of staff professionalism on deinstitutionalization, which once again conflicts with the findings of other research, can be attributed to the relative unimportance of search processes and the fact that in juvenile correctional agencies internal decision-making power is heavily concentrated in the hands of agency directors. A conclusion that takes the form of a hypothesis that interaction exists between the impact of professionalism and these two factors appears more realistic than one that assumes that this study alone has captured the "true" relationship between professionalism and innovativeness or leaves it up to future research to resolve the discrepancy between studies in an either-or fashion. Such a conclusion is also both more cumulative and more general in the sense that it takes into consideration and attempts to account for the results of other studies. Chapter 5 explored at length the substantial theoretical and empirical justification for posing such conditional hypotheses with respect to centralization, complexity, and size, which dimensions were generally assumed, until quite recently, to have a significant and consistent effect on innovativeness. Furthermore, as is clear from the examples just given, there is ample reason to believe that the impact of many of these variables is conditional on the scores of not one but several factors.

Interaction, Dimensionality, and the Future of Determinants Research

A recognition of the conditional nature of the impact of the bureaucracy and its characteristics on innovativeness helps to explain why many of the findings of the public policy and organizational innovation literatures have been so unstable. As the decision-making context (i.e., the combined characteristics of the policy innovation in question and those of its potential adopters) changes, so does the explanatory effect of many dimensions commonly included in the analysis. Yet if this sort of complex interaction is an accurate description of reality, where are we left in terms of being able to formulate even the most modest generalizations from which to make predictions about the innovativeness of organizations and polities? Can we make any statement about the determinants of innovation and their impact on organizational design without having to attach an endless series of qualifications?

Such questions cannot be resolved here, but their importance justifies speculation about where the preceding analysis has left us in terms of our ability to generalize about the determinants of policy innovation, the feasibility of developing a unitary theory of policy innovation, and the direction future research might profitably take. Of course, the emphasis placed on the contingent nature of relationships and the complexity involved should not be permitted to obscure the fact that a number of policy areas in state government are similar enough to juvenile corrections with regard to their visibility, uncertainty of outcomes, and other dimensions, to allow us to apply some portion of the findings in a fairly straightforward fashion. For example, we might expect the role of the bureaucracy (and socioeconomic heterogeneity as well) in the areas of adult corrections, foster care, vocational rehabilitation, and mental retardation to be quite similar to that in juvenile corrections—at least with respect to outputs not closely related to spending levels.

But while the value of the insights this might provide should not be minimized, it is difficult to see how we can be confident of our ability to make precise statements or generalize about the effect of specific variables on innovativeness until we know considerably more than we now do about the patterns and strength of the interaction among characteristics of the choice situation. In what has preceded we have consistently seen how far we can go astray if we assume that the results obtained in one study are directly applicable to another in which the decision to innovate is being made in a very different context. The theoretical and empirical cases for the presence of interaction cannot be ignored, and imply that nonadditive models of innovation should be constructed that explicitly recognize it.

Yet if complex interaction among variables is as common as there is reason to suspect, the development of a conceptually tractable "general" model of innovation may be almost impossible. Suppose, for instance, that the impact of organizational complexity depends on five, six, or even more other factors, including the degree of centralization, the ideological diversity of the professions involved, the communicability of the innovation in question, and its benefit-cost ratio for the groups involved. While in theory such fifth- and sixth-order interaction effects can be discovered and handled statistically, the incorporation of several variables whose impact is so unstable in any model makes great demands on sample size, greatly violates the norm of parsimony, and, as a practical matter, makes parameter estimation unfeasible.

The existence of such complex interaction means that the impact of these variables is effectively idiosyncratic to the choice situation. Thus their coefficients can be expected to vary dramatically depending on the context of the decision. Carried to its furthest extreme this implies, in the terms of the simulator, that there must be as many models as there are decision situations. Rampant interaction is evidence that we are plagued by "system interference," or the traditional functionalist dilemma [Przeworski and Teune, 1970:104; Downs, 1975]. We are faced with a situation where apparently similar characteristics of social systems perform different roles (i.e., have different impacts) across those systems (or in connection with different outputs) and, conversely, superficially disparate elements of systems may perform equivalent functions within them (or, once again, in connection with different outputs).

Fortunately, it is possible that a portion of this excessively complex interaction is a function of the type of variables included in the analyses rather than of some fundamental and immutable attribute of the behavior being studied. Possibly as a reaction to the surfeit of nebulous and operationally slippery dimensions such as "power" in traditional sociology and political science, quantitative researchers have become preoccupied with what Willer and Webster call "observables." Observables are concepts or variables "immediately susceptible to direct sensory observation and hence are often called descriptive terms" [Willer and Webster, 1970:749]. They are distinguishable from "theoretical concepts" in that the latter are abstract constructions only indicated by observable characteristics, while observables *are* those characteristics. *Status characteristic* is an example of a theoretical concept, while *laborer* or *clerk* is an observable. The distinction is not an absolute one, but the difference in the level of abstraction is certainly recognizable. One has only to look at a list of the independent variables used in the average determinants study to see that the vast majority rather unmistakably fall into the "observables" category.

While Willer and Webster do not discuss the matter, it is a fact that observables are much more subject to interaction than are theoretical concepts. Physicists speak in terms of mass (a theoretical construct) when making generalizations rather than weight (an observable) because the latter is highly susceptible to changes in position. It is always theoretically possible to specify the complex patterns of interaction among observables, but it is not often possible to do so and preserve any degree of generalizability. Because such a high proportion of the arguments linking commonly employed organizational variables with innovation contain numerous implicit assumptions of a conditional nature and therefore are likely to have an unstable effect on innovativeness, we might conclude that researchers have historically dealt with dimensions more reminiscent of weight than mass. The presence of rampant interaction among predictors should tell us that the processes of policy formation in the states (or organizations) and across policy areas are dissimilar enough to make the existing preoccupation with process and structural "observables" problematic. What might be needed are more abstract dimensions that relate to outputs in a consistent way or interact in a relatively simple fashion.

But how are we to approach this problem of dimensionality? A clustering technique such as factor analysis, at least as it is conventionally employed, is not the answer since such algorithms are based on bivariate correlations calculated across the entire population of units of analysis and are insensitive to any interaction or nonlinearities that exist.[f] For example, factor analysis would never have revealed the dimension of environmental-group interest since that dimension is based not on the fact that its component variables such as legislative, gubernatorial, or court interests are correlated with one another but on the fact that these variables have a similar impact or perform a similar function. In this case, that function was to increase the visibility of juvenile corrections.

To reach a level of generality not obtainable through the use of observables, several scholars have, a priori, aggregated their independent variables into what might be called "super-dimensions." Along these lines, Noel Boaden categorizes characteristics of a political system as *needs* that require attention, *dispositions* about the government's appropriate response, or *resources* that are available [1972]. This is reminiscent of Mohr's classification of the determinants of innovations into motivations and resources. Such categorizations are helpful in that they encourage us to think in terms of the possibilities for substitution, where a high level of one resource or disposition may compensate for (because it functions like) another. "Resources" are assumed to relate to outputs in a simple additive or multiplicative fashion, but the observables that constitute this aggregate dimension can vary from adopter to adopter, from one policy or innovation to another. The level of abstraction of these super-dimensions circumvents much of the complex interaction that would exist if the observables from which they are constructed were directly plugged into an equation. The problem with these dimensions is that they are so abstract and general that they have no clear referents. Thus their utility is limited to ex post facto analysis and their prescriptive contribution is almost nil.

Somehow we must discover dimensions that are more abstract, theoretically richer, and more stable in their impact than observables, but are not so global as to contribute little to the development of predictive theory. While there is no single, clear-cut formula for discovering such

---

[f]There are circumstances when factor analysis can be used in a manner sensitive to system interference; see Cameron et al. [1972].

dimensions, their identification may be fostered by carefully reviewing the theoretical justification for the inclusion of variables presently found in analyses. This will serve not only to uncover potential interaction due to implicit conditional assumptions but can also reveal more abstract and fundamental dimensions.

For example, in Chapter 5 we became aware of the central role that decision costs played in the arguments linking complexity to innovativeness and the fact that that hypothesized relationship was likely to be conditional because it was doubtful that the complexity would invariably lead to increased decision costs. This suggested that theory should focus directly on decision costs rather than complexity and that this dimension would have to be constructed out of different observables as the decision context shifted, or in a manner that recognizes that it could be composed of an aggregate of observables expected to have a similar impact. In this study socioeconomic heterogeneity, decision-making autonomy (here the reciprocal of decision costs), and environmental-group interest or visibility are three examples of fairly abstract dimensions created by aggregating lower-level variables believed to act in similar ways and to have a substitutable effect for each other. Moreover, each produced a substantial statistical payoff in terms of explaining variance and yielding provocative theoretical implications. One should be careful not to minimize the measurement difficulties involved in such flexible operationalizations, but given the exploratory nature of current research and the state of the art, it seems reasonable to conclude that the potential benefits of this approach outweigh the costs.

References

References

Aiken, Michael, and Robert Alford
1970 "Community Structure and Innovation." *American Political Science Review* 64:843–64.

Allison, Graham T.
1971 *Essence of Decision: Explaining the Cuban Missile Crisis*. Boston: Little, Brown.

Bahl, Roy, and Robert Saunders
1965 "Determinants of Change in State and Local Government Expenditures." *National Tax Journal* 18:50–57.

Bakal, Yitzhak (ed.)
1973 *Closing Correctional Institutions: New Strategies for Youth Services*. Lexington, Mass.: D. C. Heath, Lexington Books.

Banfield, Edward, and James Q. Wilson
1963 *City Politics*. Cambridge, Mass.: Harvard University Press.

Bauer, Raymond A., and Kenneth Gergen (eds.)
1968 *The Study of Policy Formation*. New York: Free Press.

Bauer, Raymond A., Ithiel de Sola Pool, and Lewis Anthony Dexter
1963 *American Business and Public Policy*. New York: Atherton Press.

Boaden, Neil
1971 *Urban Policy Making*. Cambridge: Cambridge University Press.

Booms, Bernard H., and James R. Halldorson
1973 "The Politics of Redistribution: A Reformation." *American Political Science Review* 67:924–33.

Braithwaite, Richard B.
1968 *Scientific Explanation*. Cambridge: Cambridge University Press.

Broach, G.
1973 "Interparty Competition, State Welfare Policies, and Nonlinear Regression." *Journal of Politics* 35:737–47.

Browning, Rufus
1970 "Innovative and Non-Innovative Decision Processes in Government Budgeting." In Sharkansky [1970b:304–34].

Burns, Tom, and G. M. Stalker
1961 *The Management of Innovation*. London: Tavistock Publications.

Cameron, David R., Stephanie Cameron, and Richard I. Hofferbert
1975 "Nonincrementalism in Public Policy: The Dynamics of Change." Paper prepared for delivery at the annual meeting of the Midwest Political Science Association (Chicago).

Cameron, David R., J. Stephen Hendricks, and Richard I. Hofferbert
1972 "Urbanization, Social Structure, and Mass Politics." *Comparative Political Studies* 5(2):259–90.

Child, John
1972 "Organizational Structure, Environment, and Performance: The Role of Strategic Choice." *Sociology* 6:2–22.

Clark, Terry N.
1968 "Community Structure, Decision Making, Budget Expenditures, and Urban Renewal in Fifty-one American Communities." *American Sociological Review* 33:576–91.

Cnudde, Charles F., and Donald McCrone
1969 "Party Competition and Welfare Policies in the American States." *American Political Science Review* 63:858–66.

Coleman, James, E. Katz, and H. Menzel
1957 "The Diffusion of an Innovation among Physicians." *Sociometry* 20(4):253–69.

Collier, David, and Richard Messick
1975 "Prerequisites Versus Diffusion: Testing Alternative Explanations of Social Security Adoption." *American Political Science Review* 69:1299–1315.

Corwin, Ronald
1969 "Patterns of Organizational Conflict." *Administrative Science Quarterly* 14:507–22.

Cowart, Andrew T.
1969 "Anti-Poverty Expenditures in the American States: A Comparative Analysis." *Midwest Journal of Political Science* 13:219–36.

Crecine, John P.
1969 *Governmental Problem Solving.* Chicago: Rand McNally.

Cutright, Phillip
1965 "Political Structure, Economic Development, and National Security Programs." *American Journal of Sociology* 70:537–50.

Cyert, Richard M., and James G. March
1963 *A Behavioral Theory of the Firm.* Englewood Cliffs, N. J.: Prentice-Hall.

Davis, Otto A., and George H. Haines
1966 "A Political Approach to a Theory of Public Expenditures: The Case of Municipalities." *National Tax Journal* 19:259–75.

Dawson, Richard F.
1967 "Social Development, Party Competition, and Policy." In William N. Chambers and Walter D. Burnham (eds.), *The American Party Systems: Stages of Political Development.* New York: Oxford University Press.

Dawson, Richard F., and James A. Robinson
    1963 "Interparty competition, economic variables, and welfare policies in the American states." *Journal of Politics* 23:265–89.

Dill, William
    1958 "Environment as an influence on managerial autonomy." *Administrative Science Quarterly* 2:409–43.

Downs, Anthony
    1967 *Inside Bureaucracy.* Boston: Little, Brown.

Downs, George
    1975 "Interaction and the Functionalist Dilemma." Discussion paper, University of Michigan, Ann Arbor.

Downs, George, and Lawrence B. Mohr
    1976 "Conceptual Issues in the Study of Innovation." *Administrative Science Quarterly* 21(4):forthcoming.

Duncan, Robert
    1971 "The Effects of Perceived Environmental Uncertainty on Organizational Decision Unit Structure: A Cybernetic Model." Ph.D. dissertation, Yale University, New Haven, Conn.

Dye, Thomas R.
    1965 "Malapportionment and Public Policy in the States." *Journal of Politics* 37:586–601.
    1966 *Politics, Economics, and the Public: Policy Outcomes in the American States.* Chicago: Rand McNally.
    1967 "Governmental Structure, Urban Environment, and Educational Policy." *Midwest Journal of Political Science* 11:353–80.
    1969 "Income Inequality and American State Politics." *American Political Science Review* 63:157–62.

Dye, Thomas R., and N. Pollack
    1973 "Path Analytic Models in Policy Research." *Policy Studies Journal* 2:123–30.

Elazar, Daniel J.
    1966 *American Federalism: A View from the States.* New York: Thomas Y. Crowell.

Elliott, James R.
    1965 "A Comment on Inter-Party Competition, Economic Variables, and Welfare Policies in the American States." *Journal of Politics* 27:185–91.

Emery, F. E., and E. L. Trist
    1965 "The Causal Texture of Organizational Environments." *Human Relations* 18(1):21–32.

Eulau, Heinz, and Robert Eyestone
    1968 "Policy Maps of City Councils and Policy Outcomes: A De-

velopmental Analysis." *American Political Science Review* 62:124–43.

Fabricant, Solomon
 1952   *The Trend of Government Activity in the United States since 1900*. New York: National Bureau of Economic Research.

Falcone, David, and Michael Whittington
 1972   "Output Change in Canada: A Preliminary Attempt to Open the 'Black Box.' " Paper presented to CPSA (Montreal).

Fenton, John H., and Donald W. Chamberlayne
 1969   "The Literature Dealing with the Relationships between Political Processes, Socioeconomic Conditions, and Public Policies in the American States: A Bibliographic Essay." *Polity* 1:388–404.

Fisher, F. M., and A. Ando
 1962   "Two Theorems on *Ceteris Paribus* in the Analysis of Dynamic Systems." *American Political Science Review* 61 (March):103–13.

Fisher, Glenn W.
 1961   "Determinants of State and Local Government Expenditures: A Preliminary Analysis." *National Tax Journal* 14:345–55.
 1964   "Interstate Variation in State and Local Government Expenditure." *National Tax Journal* 17:57–75.

Florida Division of Youth Services
 1974   *Comprehensive Plan, 1974–80*. Tallahassee.

Fried, Robert C.
 1973   "Comparative urban performance." European Urban Research Working Paper, no. 1, University of California, Los Angeles.

Friedman, Lee
 1973   "Innovation and Diffusion in Non-Markets: Case Studies in Criminal Justice." Ph.D. dissertation, Yale University, New Haven, Conn.

Friedman, Milton
 1953   *Essays in Positive Economics*. Chicago: University of Chicago Press.

Froman, Lewis A.
 1967   "An Analysis of Public Policies in Cities." *Journal of Politics* 29:94–108.
 1968   "The Categorization of Policy Contents." In Ranney [1968].

Fry, Brian R., and Richard F. Winters
 1970   "The Politics of Redistribution." *American Political Science Review* 64:508–22.

Glaser, Barney, and Anselm Strauss
 1967   *The Discovery of Grounded Theory: Strategies for Qualitative Research*. Chicago: Aldine Publishing Co.

139

Gray, Virginia
1973 "Innovation in the States: A Diffusion Study." *American Political Science Review* 67 (Dec.):1174–85.
Gray, Virginia, and John Wanat
1974 "Public Policies in the American States: New Formulations of Old Problems." Paper presented at the annual meeting of the Midwest Political Science Association (Chicago).
Griliches, Zvi
1957 "Hybrid Corn—An Exploration in the Economies of Technological Change." *Econometrica* 25(4):501–22.
1960 "Congruence versus Profitability: A False Dichotomy." *Rural Sociology* 25(3):354–56.
Hage, Jerald, and Michael Aiken
1967 "Program Change and Organizational Properties: A Comparative Analysis." *American Journal of Sociology* 72(5):503–19.
1970 *Social Change in Complex Organizations*. New York: Random House.
Hage, Jerald, and Robert Dewar
1973 "Elite Values versus Organizational Structure in Predicting Innovation." *Administrative Science Quarterly* 18(3):279–89.
Hofferbert, Richard I.
1966a "The Relationship between Public Policy and Some Structural and Environmental Variables in the American States." *American Political Science Review* 60:73–82.
1966b "Ecological Development and Policy Change in the American States." *Midwest Journal of Political Science* 10:464–83.
1968 "Socio-economic Dimensions of the American States: 1890–1960." *Midwest Journal of Political Science* 12:401–18.
1970 "Elite Influence in State Policy Formation: A Model for Comparative Inquiry." *Polity* 2:316–44.
1972 "State and Community Policy Studies." In James A. Robinson (ed.), *Political Science Annual* 3:1–72.
Jacob, Herbert, and Michael Lipsky
1968 "Outputs, Structure, and Power: An Assessment of Changes in the Study of State and Local Politics." *Journal of Politics* 30:510–38.
Jacob, Herbert, and Kenneth N. Vines (eds.)
1965 *Politics in the American States*. Boston: Little, Brown.
1971 *Politics in the American States—A Comparative Analysis*. 2nd ed. Boston: Little, Brown.
Kamien, M., and N. Schwartz
1975 "Market Structure and Innovation: A Survey." *Journal of Economic Literature* 13(1):1–37.

Kessel, John H.
1962   "Government Structure and Political Environment: A Statistical
        Note about American Cities." *American Political Science Review* 56:615–20.
Key, V. O., Jr.
1949   *Southern Politics*. New York: Alfred A. Knopf.
Kurnow, Ernest
1963   "Determinants of State and Local Expenditures Reexamined."
        National Tax Journal 16:252–55.
La Palombara, J.
1968   "Macrotheories and Microapplications in Comparative Politics:
        A Widening Chasm." *Comparative Politics* 1:52–78.
Larkey, Patrick
1975   "Process Models and Program Evaluation: The Impact of General Revenue Sharing on Municipal Fiscal Behavior." Ph.D.
        dissertation, University of Michigan, Ann Arbor.
Lawrence, Paul, and Jay Lorsch
1967   *Organization and Environment*. Cambridge: Harvard University
        Press.
LeMay, Michael
1973   "Expenditure and Nonexpenditure Measures of State Urban
        Policy Output: A Research Note." *American Politics Quarterly,*
        October: 511–27.
Lineberry, Robert L., and Edmund P. Fowler
1967   "Reformism and Public Policies in American Cities." *American
        Political Science Review* 61:701–16.
Lipset, Seymour Martin, and Stein Rokkan (eds.)
1967   *Party Systems and Voter Alignments*. New York: Free Press.
Lockard, Duane
1968   "State Party Systems and Policy Outputs." In Oliver Garceau
        (ed.), *Political Research and Political Theory*. Cambridge,
        Mass.: Harvard University Press.
Lowi, Theodore
1964   "American Business, Public Policy, Case Studies, and Political
        Theory." *World Politics* 6:677–715.
1969   *The End of Liberalism*. New York: Norton.
Loy, John
1969   "Social Psychological Characteristics of Innovators." *American
        Sociological Review* 34(1):73–82.
Mansfield, Edwin
1961   "Technical Change and the Rate of Imitation." *Econometrica*
        29(4):741–66.

1963a   "The Speed of Response of Firms to New Techniques." *Quarterly Journal of Economics* 77(2):290–309.

1963b   "Intrafirm Rates of Diffusion of an Innovation." *Review of Economic Statistics* 45(4):348–59.

1963c   "Size of Firm, Market Structure, and Innovation." *Journal of Political Economy* 71(6):557–76.

1968a   *The Economics of Technological Change.* New York: Norton.

1968b   *Industrial Research and Technological Innovation—An Econometric Analysis.* New York: Norton.

Mansfield, E., J. Rapoport, J. Schnee, S. Wagner, and M. Hamburger
1971   *Research and Innovation in the Modern Corporation.* New York: Norton.

March, James, and Herbert Simon
1958   *Organizations.* New York: Wiley.

McGee, Richard A.
1971   "The Organizational Structure of State and Local Correctional Services." *Public Administration Review* 31:616–21.

Miner, Jerry
1963   *Social and Economic Factors in Spending for Public Education.* Syracuse, N.Y.: Syracuse University Press.

Mohr, Lawrence B.
1969   "Determinants of Innovation in Organizations." *American Political Science Review* 64:111–26.

1971   "Organizational Technology and Organizational Structure." *Administrative Science Quarterly* 16(4):444–59.

Morris, Norval
1970   Foreword to *Halfway Houses: Community-Centered Correction and Treatment,* by Oliver J. Keller, Jr., and Benedict S. Alper. Lexington, Mass.: D.C. Heath, Lexington Books.

Morss, Eliott
1966   "Some Thoughts on the Determinants of State and Local Expenditures." *National Tax Journal* 19:95–104.

National Advisory Commission on Criminal Justice Standards and Goals
1973   *Corrections.* Washington, D.C.: Government Printing Office.

Nelson, Richard
1965   "The Allocation of Research and Development Resources: Some Problems of Public Policy." In Tybout [1965].

1972   "Issues and Suggestions for the Study of Industrial Organization in a Regime of Rapid Technical Change." In V. Fuchs (ed.), *Policy Issues and Research Opportunities in Industrial Organization.* National Bureau of Economic Research. New York: Columbia University Press.

1973a "Neoclassical vs. Evolutionary Theories of Economic Growth: Critique and Prospectus." Institute of Public Policy Studies Discussion Paper, no. 46, University of Michigan, Ann Arbor.

1973b "Toward an Evolutionary Theory of Economic Capabilities." *American Economic Review* 63:440–49.

Nelson, Richard, and Sidney Winter
1975 "Growth Theory from an Evolutionary Perspective: The Differential Productivity Puzzle." *American Economic Review* 65(2):330–44.

Nelson, R., S. Winter, and H. Schuette
1973 "Technical Change in an evolutionary model." Institute of Public Policy Studies Discussion Paper, no. 45, University of Michigan, Ann Arbor.

Neubauer, Deane
1967 "Some Conditions of Democracy." *American Political Science Review* 61:1002–09.

Niskanen, William A.
1971 *Bureaucracy and Representative Government.* Chicago: Aldine-Atherton.

Nozick, Robert
1974 *Anarchy, State, and Utopia.* New York: Basic Books.

Olsen, Marvin E.
1968 "Multivariate Analysis of National Political Development." *American Sociological Review* 33:699–711.

Peters, B. Guy
1972 "Public Policy, Socioeconomic Conditions, and the Political System: A Note on Their Developmental Relationship." Research notes.

President's Commission on Law Enforcement and Administration of Justice
1967 *Task Force Report: Juvenile Delinquency and Youth Crime.* Washington, D.C.: Government Printing Office.

Pryor, Frederick L.
1968 *Public Expenditures in Communist and Capitalist Nations.* London: Allen & Unwin.

Przeworski, Adam, and Henry Teune
1970 *The Logic of Comparative Social Inquiry.* New York: John Wiley.

Quay, Herbert C.
1973 "What Corrections Can Correct and How." *Federal Probation* 37(2):3–5.

Ranney, Austin (ed.)
1968 *Political Science and Public Policy.* Chicago: Markham.

Ripley, Randal B. (ed.)
  1966 *Public Policies and Their Politics*. New York: W. W. Norton.
Rogers, Everett
  1962 *Diffusion of Innovations*. New York: Free Press.
Rogers, Everett, and Floyd Shoemaker
  1971 *Communication of Innovations—A Cross-cultural Approach*. New York: Free Press.
Rokkan, Stein
  1968 *Comparative Research across Cultures and Nations*. The Hague: Mouton.
  1969 *Comparative Survey Analysis*. The Hague: Mouton.
  1970 *Citizens, Elections, Parties*. New York: McKay.
Rourke, Francis E.
  1969 *Bureaucracy, Politics, and Public Policy*. Boston: Little, Brown.
Sacks, Seymour, and Robert Harris
  1964 "The Determinants of State and Local Government Expenditures and Intergovernmental Flows of Funds." *National Tax Journal* 17:75–85.
Salisbury, Robert H.
  1968 "The Analysis of Public Policy: A Search for Theories and Roles." In Ranney [1968].
Salisbury, Robert H., and John Heinz
  1970 "A Theory of Policy Analysis and Some Preliminary Applications." In Sharkansky [1970b].
Sapolsky, Harvey
  1967 "Organizational Structure and Innovation." *Journal of Business* 40(4):497–510.
Sargent, Francis W.
  1973 "Community-based Treatment for Juveniles in Massachusetts." In *New Approaches to Diversion and Treatment of Juvenile Offenders*. National Institute of Law Enforcement and Criminal Justice monograph. Washington, D.C.: Government Printing Office.
Scherer, Frederic M.
  1970 *Industrial Market Structure and Economic Performance*. Chicago: Rand McNally.
Schlesinger, Joseph A.
  1965 "The Politics of the Executive." In Jacob and Vines [1965].
Schubert, Glendon, and Charles Press
  1964 "Measuring Malapportionment." *American Political Science Review* 63:302–27.
Schumpeter, Joseph A.

1950 *Capitalism, Socialism and Democracy.* New York: Harper & Bros.

1969 *The Theory of Economic Development.* New York: Oxford University Press.

Selznick, Philip

1949 *TVA and the Grass Roots.* Berkeley: University of California Press.

1957 *Leadership in Administration.* Evanston, Ill.: Row, Peterson.

Sharkansky, Ira

1967a "Economic and Political Correlates of State Government Expenditures." Midwest Journal of Political Science 11:173–92.

1967b "Government Expenditures and Public Policies in the American States." *American Political Science Review* 61:1066–77.

1968 "Economic Development, Regionalism, and State Political Systems." *Midwest Journal of Political Science* 12:41–61.

1969 "The Utility of Elazar's Political Culture: A Research Note." *Polity* 2(Fall):66–84.

1970a "Environment, Policy, Output, and Impact: Problems of Theory and Method in the Analysis of Public Policy." In Sharkansky [1970b].

1970b (ed.) *Policy Analysis in Political Science.* Chicago: Markham.

Sharkansky, Ira, and Richard I. Hofferbert

1969 "Dimensions of State Politics, Economics, and Public Policy." *American Political Science Review* 63:867–80.

Simon, Herbert A.

1968 "On Judging the Plausibility of Theories." In J. van Rootselaar and H. Stall (eds.), *Logic, Methodology and Philosophy of Sciences* 3:439–59. Amsterdam: North Holland Publishing Co.

1969 *The Sciences of the Artificial.* Cambridge, Mass.: MIT Press.

Simon, Herbert A., and A. Ando

1961 "Aggregation of Variables in Dynamic Systems." *Econometrica* 29(April):111–38.

Stinchcombe, Arthur

1965 "Social Structure and Organizations." In James G. March (ed.), *Handbook of Organizations.* Chicago: Rand McNally.

Strouse, J., and J. O. Williams

1972 "A Non-Additive Model for State Policy Research." *Journal of Politics* 34:648–61.

Terreberry, Shirley

1968 "The Evolution of Organizational Environments." *Administrative Science Quarterly* 12:590–613.

Thompson, James D.

1967 *Organizations in Action.* New York: McGraw-Hill.

Thompson, Victor A.

1969   *Bureaucracy and Innovation*. University: University of Alabama Press.

Tybout, R. (ed.)
   1965   *Economics of Research and Development*. Columbus: Ohio State University Press.

U.S. National Criminal Justice Information and Statistics Service
   1974   *Children in Custody: A Report on the Juvenile Detention and Correctional Facility Census of 1971*. Washington, D.C.: Law Enforcement Assistance Administration.

Van Meter, D., and H. Asher
   1973   "Causal Analysis: Its Promise for Policy Studies." *Policy Studies Journal* 2:103–9.

Vinter, Robert D., with George Downs
   1974   "State Juvenile Justice Systems: A Preliminary Report." Paper delivered at the Academy for Contemporary Problems conference on "The Politics of Correctional Change," Columbus, Ohio.

Vinter, Robert D., George Downs, and John Hall
   1975   *Juvenile Corrections in the States: Residential Programs and Deinstitutionalization*. Ann Arbor: National Assessment of Juvenile Corrections.

Walker, Jack L.
   1969   "The Diffusion of Innovations among the American States." *American Political Science Review* 63:880–99.
   1971   "Innovations in State Politics." In Jacob and Vines [1971].

Warner, Kenneth
   1974   "The Need for Some Innovative Concepts of Innovation: An Examination of Research on the Diffusion of Innovations." *Policy Sciences* 5:443–51.

Weber, Max
   1968   *Economy and Society*. Vols. 1 and 3. Edited by Guenther Roth and Claus Wittich. New York: Bedminster Press.

Willer, David, and Murray Webster
   1970   "Theoretical Concepts and Observables." *American Sociological Review* 35:748–57.

Wilson, James Q.
   1966   "Innovation and Organization: Notes toward a Theory." In James Thompson (ed.), *Approaches to Organizational Design*. Pittsburgh, Pa.: University of Pittsburgh Press.

Winter, Sidney
   1971   "Satisficing, Selection and the Innovating Remnant." *Quarterly Journal of Economics* 85(2):237–61.

Zaltman, Gerald, Robert Duncan, and Jonny Holbek
   1973   *Innovations and Organizations*. New York: Wiley.

Index

147

About the Author

George W. Downs, Jr. received the Ph.D. from the University of Michigan and teaches public policy and organizational behavior in the Department of Political Science at the University of California, Davis. He has previously written on innovation in complex organizations, interaction and dimensionality in comparative policy analysis, and juvenile corrections policy. Professor Downs is working on a project sponsored by the National Science Foundation to overcome a number of the theoretical and methodological problems connected with innovation research. In addition, he is coauthoring a book on correctional policy making and has recently initiated exploratory research on stochastic models of social networks.